How to Be a
Perfect Wife
and
Other Myths

How to Be a Perfect Wife and Other Myths

AFTON DAY

BOOKCRAFT, INC.
Salt Lake City, Utah

Library of Congress Catalog Card Number: 77-75313
ISBN 0-88494-317-8

2nd Printing, 1977

Lithographed in the United States of America
PUBLISHERS PRESS
Salt Lake City, Utah

Contents

Preface vii

1 Far Above Rubies   1

2 I Am Only One, But I Am One   8

3 Honor the Priesthood: Potent or Potential 22

4 The Art of Being First Counselor 32

5 Constructive Coexistence 38

6 Robots, Parrots, or Personalities? 49

7 The Sixth September 57

8 Got Your Ears On? 68

9 Nobody Wins in a Power Struggle 75

10 The Magic Potatoes 85

11 We're All in This Thing Together 96

12 Hold Tight and Hang Loose 105

Preface

◇○◁━━━━━━━━━━━━━━━━━━━━

"If you live the gospel, things will turn out all right." When I was a child, living the gospel meant the Word of Wisdom and going to church. As I grew older, it was dress standards and making it to the temple. From then on, I imagined, it had to be downhill all the way.

What a shock to realize that my adult mind didn't automatically stop questioning, and to find that in order to really live the gospel I had to give up some of the prejudices I had felt so comfortable with before! And what a blow to discover that, even when I felt I had laid them to rest mentally, they would insist on periodically peeping up through the emotions!

I have tried in this book to share some of the insights that have resulted from the years of questions, readjustments, and changes of focus. I hope I have done so in a way that will reach out to others who, like me, have perfection as a goal but a yet imperfect mind and body as a vehicle.

This book is dedicated:
  To my husband, Sherman, with gratitude for his patience and long-suffering.
  To Bradley, the nine-year-old sage who keeps us all on the straight and narrow.
  To Kristin, my beautiful and organized daughter.
From my father, the late Hans C. Jensen, I received inspiration for the chapter "I Am Only One, But I Am One."

Chapter 1
Far Above Rubies

"Who can find a virtuous woman? for her price is far above rubies. The heart of her husband doth safely trust in her, . . . She will do him good and not evil all the days of her life. She seeketh wool, and flax, and worketh willingly with her hands. . . ." (Proverbs 31:10-13.)

Willingly? My mind is wandering. I picture the drawer full of mending, and the material I bought to make my second-grader a dress the year she entered kindergarten. *But I love to cook. . . .*

It's Mother's Day, and I am in Sunday School. Another year has passed, and still I don't see any resemblance between myself and the mothers they talk about, those adoring husbands and children speaking in turn from the pulpit. One middle-aged man has read a tribute to a soft-spoken mother who had never, in his recollection, raised her voice. A loving husband has complimented his wife on never having worn her hair in curlers in his presence. Wretch that I am, I have become defensive. *I'll bet she has naturally curly hair and he doesn't know it!*

There is a rustling sound, like an army of innocents being called to order, and I realize that the Junior Sunday School is about to sing. My troubled brow relaxes and my lips form a smile. The Junior Sunday School's offering is consistently the highlight of the Mother's Day program. I open my purse and search desperately among the gum wrappers and sales slips for a clean handkerchief. A fresh Kleenex. *Any* Kleenex. . . .

The children sing "Mother, I Love You," and "Mother Dear." They are all beautiful — even Jimmy-down-the-street, who picked all my tulips this morning. My daughter looks angelic as she sneaks in a little wave between verses. My, but she's grown just since Easter! Her floor-length dress now reveals scuffed-up saddle shoes and a glimpse of Woody Woodpecker knee-lengths. My tears flow freely now; the children are well into their third and final offering. It is a challenge no mother can resist, sung so fervently with just a hint of baby talk:

> "I am a child of God,
> And so my needs are great.
> Help me to understand his words
> Before it grows too late."

I glance across the aisle at my nine-year-old, attentive and reverent in his bow tie and wash-and-wear Sunday clothes. He needs a haircut. He looks at me, then quickly away. It embarrasses him to see his mother cry in public.

> "Lead me, guide me, walk beside me.
> Help me find the way.
> Teach me all that I must do
> To live with him some day."

The congregation is hushed, and even fathers are seen wiping their eyes and noses. This is one message that can't escape us, any of us. It's moments like this which make the dirty diapers and the PTA meetings all worthwhile. And it's moments like this which compel every mother to make a silent resolution: "I'll do better, Heavenly Father, with thy help."

Why is it that Mother's Day speeches depress me? And why, even in the Church, where motherhood and woman-hood are held in such high esteem, do many of us still experience feelings of depression, inferiority, lack of ful-fillment, and boredom? Perhaps the problem is one of point of view. While the poets, the scriptures, and all who speak and write about the beauty of womanhood are describing forests, we women are doggedly trying to find the best path amongst an overwhelming number of trees!

For example, when the Psalmist, in praising the goodness of the Lord, says, "He maketh the barren woman to keep house, and to be a joyful mother of children" (Psalm 113:9), he doesn't mention that, even though the barren woman is probably overjoyed at the blessing of children, there might be things about the keeping of the house that cause her occa-sional panic or at least frustration. Those observations just aren't Psalm material! And it's only natural for a poet to prefer to write about the soft, sweet moments of motherhood than about the telephoning responsibilities of a team mother or the tedium of driving a carpool. Such an option, unrealistic as it may at times seem, is covered under the rights and liberties of poetic licence.

An occasional look at the whole, or the forest, can be encouraging and inspiring. The feeling I get when I hear a group of children singing "I Am a Child of God" is similar to the thrill I feel when I sing the "Messiah," witness a temple sealing, or attend a missionary farewell or an inspir-ing fireside. Moments like these allow me to stand back and see eternity in perspective. But without the sometimes te-dious, sometimes demanding everyday tasks, the peak ex-periences become spectator sports instead of actual glimpses into a celestial future.

Ever since I was a young girl, I have believed that being a mother sitting on the stand listening to her newly-called missionary son[1] deliver his farewell address would be just about the most thrilling thing in the world. There's something about the picture of that young man, fighting tears as he admits that his parents weren't such dopes after all, that gives me goosebumps.

I still get just as excited at missionary farewells as I did when I was younger, but now I realize that in addition to setting a good example and teaching gospel principles, in order to see a young man to his nineteenth year a mother would have had to change at least 9,125 diapers; attend (often anxiously) at least 220 little league games (if you include football or soccer, basketball, and baseball); use hundreds of gallons of gas and many more hours of time transporting her son to practices, music lessons, Primary, and/or other activities; agonize over a first date (and, even worse, over subsequent ones), a voice change, and a multitude of growing pains; and cook thousands of filling as well as nutritious meals. And what is even more sobering, as I look around me I realize that many fine women go through all the steps I have mentioned and never have the privilege of sending a boy or girl on a mission. In fact, some young people from worthy families do not choose to accept their parents' teachings and sometimes don't admit until much later in life that their parents are all-right people.

The conscientious and well-informed Latter-day Saint woman may find herself overwhelmed by the number of demands on her time or may have moments of frustration owing to a conflict of priorities. We are told "Be ye therefore perfect" (Matthew 5:48) and "Men are, that they might have joy" (2 Nephi 2:25). Help the poor, sick, and needy. Do your visiting teaching, magnify your calling, but don't neglect community and neighborhood activities. Plant a garden, freeze and can, prepare for the future, but seize the teaching opportunity that never comes again. Keep your home clean

---

[1]My apologies to missionary daughters, who are just as beautiful, for the choice of this example. When I was growing up, not many girls became missionaries.

and orderly, but never let your husband or children feel that your work is more important than they are. Keep yourself attractive and interesting, but don't be selfish with your time. Accept responsibilities willingly, but never neglect your family. And so on.

If you're one of those women who manage to do all of the above on Monday through Saturday and then come to church on Sunday morning looking rested and radiant in a home-sewn dress that could have come from the Designer Dress Department, thank your friends or family for giving you this book and then discreetly pass it on to your visiting teacher when she comes by on the thirtieth. You don't need it. If you belong to the other 99 percent you have a choice: Either cop out, or cope.

If you have chosen the first, reconsider. There are a tragic few who find the rules so difficult to follow that they opt to either leave the Church, become inactive, stay active but revise the rules, or, in extreme cases, leave the family. These are options from an earthly point of view only. Viewed from an eternal perspective such approaches must be listed under "L" for "loser."

So because of our love for our families and the undeniable knowledge that there *is* a life after death, somehow we cope. At times we achieve, we soar, we transcend the mundane. But at other times we simply cope. This is not to undermine the quality of our devotion to our families or to the gospel; it is just another way of saying that sometimes love is sharing the grief of a four-year-old at the burial of a dead turtle instead of composing a song about the joys of motherhood.

Being a mother lends itself to introspection. I've analyzed many problems and situations while doing the ironing and cleaning the mildew on the shower tiles. I've made an amazing number of profound observations during a few precious quiet times spent with a child and a rocking chair, only to find the next day that my conclusions had not withstood the test of time. There are a few ideas, however, that have developed during my sixteen years of being a wife and my nine years of being a mother that seem to have given me some strength and encouragement.

Regarding the problem of how to do all that is expected of us and how to live up to the rigid standard of LDS womanhood, I've observed that from a tree-watcher's point of view there seems to be a fine line between complacency and contentment. While I have no authority to make judgment, I am convinced that our Father in heaven has a great love for each of us, no matter what our present state and no matter what our problems or habits may be. Whether a woman is feeling a need for help because she is recently divorced or because she is constantly disorganized, an unbelievable amount of heavenly love and assistance is available. At any stage of development we may concur with Nephi that ''the Lord giveth no commandments unto the children of men, save he shall prepare a way for them that they may accomplish the thing which he commandeth them.'' (1 Nephi 3:7.) Our Father in heaven has faith in our ability to do what has to be done. If only we had as much confidence in ourselves!

I've concluded that it's all right to be imperfect; but it's not all right to settle for imperfection. It's okay (it's imperative!) to accept yourself; but it's not okay to be self-satisfied. Each level of progression up the ladder of spirituality brings increased rewards — the kind of rewards you can feel and use in your everyday life, not just an added wing to your heavenly mansion. Success builds upon success, and common sense tells me that as we increase our spirituality life becomes more stimulating, if not easier, and our capacity for love becomes greater.

Count the ways you show love for your family: Making formula late at night when your muscles ache with exhaustion? Staying up until two in the morning to work on that special prom dress? Letting your three-year-old spill more milk on the table than he pours into his glass because you know he needs the confidence that helping himself brings? Resisting the urge to say ''I told you so'' to your husband? There are hundreds of ways, even though they may not be the ones that will win you a nomination for Mother of the Year!

So let's join forces in an attempt to make our lives and those of our families more joyful by ridding ourselves of self-criticism and discouragement while we seek to improve the quality of our mother-love by increasing our human relations skills and moving up the ladder of spirituality. Next time you attend a Mother's Day program, accept your potted geranium proudly — you've earned it. Then nourish it with humility, as you will continue to nourish your own soul and the souls of your precious family.

Chapter 2

I Am Only One,
But I Am One

⎯◇o⎯⎯⎯⎯⎯⎯⎯⎯⎯⎯⎯⎯⎯⎯⎯⎯⎯⎯⎯⎯

I went from a happy, confident child to a real Nowhere teenager. I wasn't rebellious, nor did I really withdraw — I just sort of blended in with the dull grey lockers that lined the walls of our junior high. My family and teachers tried everything to convince me that I was cute, talented, likeable, and bright, but I outsmarted them all by remaining dull and ordinary.

By the time I reached high school the miserable doubts of adolesence were beginning to disappear, but a student leader I was not, by any stretch of the imagination. It was with great surprise and delight that I learned during the summer following my junior year that there had been a last-minute cancellation and I had been nominated and approved to attend the Girls' Club Leadership Camp in Big Cottonwood Canyon.

That was over twenty years ago, and I've long since forgotten whether the Girls' Club ever served any worthwhile function, or whether I was ever invited back again. But I've never forgotten an experience I had at that camp.

The main attraction of the convention was the presence of Elaine Cannon, at that time the Salt Lake Valley teenagers' answer to Amy Vanderbilt, Ann Landers, and Art Buchwald. Even now, with the highly respected *Washington Post* delivered to my home every day, I don't read anything with the vigor and devotion with which I then digested her "Hi Tales" column.

So, needless to say, I was impressed and overjoyed to discover that Mrs. Cannon had chosen to speak on overcoming feelings of inadequacy. Could it be true that other girls of my age group felt inadequate, too? Or had she been inspired to choose this subject just for me? I remember vividly sitting on a long log-bench and copying words of wisdom which went something like this:

> I am only one,
> But I *am* one.
> I can't do everything,
> But I *can* do something.
> And what I can do,
> With the help of God
> I *will* do.

What lessons are contained in that short quotation! The admission of humility, along with the recognition of personal power. The beauty of self-direction, along with the admission of need for heavenly help. I've forgotten every algebraic equation I learned in high school; I've even forgotten how to diagram a sentence. But the power of that quotation has stayed in my mind these many years, and I hope I can pass on its wisdom to my own children and others whom I am called upon to teach.

If you were allowed to teach only one thing to your children, what would you choose? A love of the gospel? Respect for others? Responsibility? It would be a difficult choice to make. After much serious consideration, I believe that if I were allowed to give only one thing to my children, I would choose to give them a positive self-concept — a feeling of worth and self-respect.

How do I dare make such a statement? I guess it's because, looking around me (and within myself), I've noticed that other teachings don't always bear the fruits they should if they are planted in a field of self-doubt or self-abasement. For example, many young people are led to the use of drugs and alcohol or even to sexual promiscuity not because they especially want to do those things but because they feel a desperate need to fit into a peer group. Others use those things to escape from a world in which they just don't feel they can measure up to what is expected of them. Many marriages end in disaster because one or both of the partners are so desperately seeking for their own needs to be met that they don't know how to satisfy the needs of another. And even when no massive problems arise, it is impossible to gain the celestial level we are seeking, or the joy the scriptures advocate, with a soul filled with doubt and recrimination.

But the slogan of the Church's Youth Posters of several years ago holds painfully true in this case. ''Be Honest With Yourself — Nothing Worth Having Is Free.'' If the good gifts are gained after much seeking and toil, certainly a positive self-concept is one of the most difficult to teach. Difficult because our children receive messages of ''I'm good'' or ''I'm bad'' in *every* interaction with *everyone*, not just at those times when we are prepared to teach. Difficult, too, because like so many of the principles of right living, self-esteem is taught best by example.

I used to teach the Church Parent Education Course with my husband, and somehow or other he always happened to be out of town when the lesson on self-esteem came up. I was supposed to show that the first way to teach self-esteem was through example. I always drew a blank. How does a mother or father, with the usual number of guilt feelings, doubts, and failures that most of us acquire by the time we reach adulthood, set an example of self-esteem? It makes one stop and think.

Is your own lack of self-esteem a problem? Perhaps not. Generally people don't like to discuss this subject. I have heard many women complain of the housewife doldrums, being too busy, having lost control of their children, or resenting things their husbands do or expect *them* to do, but not many complain of having a lousy self-image. Maybe I'm the only one who suffers periodic attacks of this malady.

On the assumption that someone will identify with my observation, however, I confess that most of the time when I suffer from cabin fever, overwork, lack of time, obnoxious children, or an unreasonable husband, I am usually feeling a serious lack of self-esteem. In fact, a low self-image has been my greatest enemy in my endeavor to become the successful woman, wife, and mother I have always planned to be.

Let me describe myself when I like me. I'm excited about *everything*! I can even remember feeling absolutely euphoric while cleaning my filthy kitchen ceiling. I feel that I can conquer anything — even the urge to finish off the peach pie after dinner. It's like the feeling I used to get when tubing down the mountainside in the freezing winter air, warmed only by the glow of my red cheeks and the excitement I felt in the pit of my stomach.

And when I don't like myself, it's the blahs. I enjoy eating and sleeping more than working. I shy away from contact with people, but I end up missing it. I get bored and cynical, and I worry about problems that the confident me could handle easily.

For an adult, what helps to create a positive self-image? As I try to pinpoint situations or events, I find that the success-failure story is circular. Does achievement bring about self-esteem or does self-esteem bring about achievement? Am I happier because I try new things, or do I have to come to a certain level of peace with myself in order to *dare* to try new things? The cause and effect seem to be inseparable. As I look back, I see that the high points in my life are all connected with new challenges: my four years at college, the beginning of my teaching career, falling in love, graduate school, and the adoption of my children. The low points, on the other hand, seem to have either the absence of a new challenge or the presence of a challenge that I hadn't chosen: adolescence; the period of time after I had stopped working and after I had established a routine existence at home; a move; and, connected with that move, the anti-climax of having both my children in school.

Finding the beginning of a circle is rather like grasping the brass ring on the merry-go-round. It is futile to spend time trying to determine which is the beginning and which is the end. The best way to break into a circle is to find a point — any point — and get on the track.

For example, when I find that things are getting out of hand and I need to change my downward course to an upward one, I can be pretty sure that an improvement in either my spirituality, physical fitness, or level of achievement will bring about, or at least *begin* to bring about, the desired result. If I can control my diet, jog for fifteen minutes a day, and keep my hair looking decent, I usually find that my spirituality increases and my mental outlook is brightened considerably. But if I can't quite bring myself to get out of bed or out of the house to jog, and if I find it impossible to control my ravenous appetite, I can make it a habit to have regular and serious prayer and/or scripture reading and thus eventually get the strength and willpower to do my jogging or dieting. And if a new challenge, such as taking a class (or teaching one), is added, the mental and social stimulation usually increases my motivation to improve both my spirit and my body.

If it's important for a mother to maintain a positive self-image, it's equally important that the father in the home sets an example of confidence and self-esteem. The feeling of mutual respect — no, more than respect, *admiration* — between a husband and wife is of tremendous importance in a family.

Everyone needs to feel loved; everyone needs to feel important. *Boy, does everyone need to feel loved and important!* We probably don't realize how much we need this until we see what happens to people when they are unable to find love and attention in their own homes. Husbands, although they may be more mature and better able to deal with feelings of rejection, need attention and encouragement no less (sometimes more!) than children. There are many ways a wife can encourage and build her husband; there are many ways in which she may unconsciously discourage him or put him down. Some of them will be discussed in the next chapter.

Besides example, how do we teach a child to feel good about himself? Probably we are not conscious of most of the cues we give: smiling, cuddling, sighing, moaning, frowning. The child reads fairly accurately every message we send, so the one who is really wanted and loved is bound to receive more positive cues than the one who is, ever-so-subtly, resented and therefore rejected. This probably accounts for the fact that some people who seem to do everything wrong according to the "how-to" books have happy, confident children, while others who know all the answers have unhappy, anxious ones.

There are, however, a few very conscious things that we as mothers can do to help our children to grow in confidence and self-esteem. Probably all of them can be classified under "Encouragement."

Remember how, when you used to play house, being "mother" meant having the authority to boss, to admonish, and to control your dolls and younger playmates? "Don't get your feet wet!" "Now look what you've done!" "How many times do I have to tell you . . .?"

Now we're grown up, and we're not just dealing with a doll which might be Shirley Temple today and Margaret O'Brien tomorrow. We're dealing with little people; specifically, with a child who might be our baby today and a young person struggling to find his or her place in a very complex, very discouraging world tomorrow. We're dealing with children whose need for love and acceptance is never satiated but whose capacities to love and share grow as they are showered with love and encouragement. Not showered with laxity and permissiveness, because in administering love and encouragement generously we sometimes need to restrain, to express displeasure, or, even more difficult, to allow the loved one to suffer unpleasant consequences.

Probably the most powerful tool for encouragement available to a mother is her own time. That has been well established; with each new day, it seems that the Church places more and more emphasis on spending time with our families. Neither is it a new idea to suggest that some time be spent with each child alone. But I had an experience not long ago which helped me to see that not all parents understand the kind of "together-time" which qualifies as encouragement.

Several years ago I was a group leader in a parent discussion group sponsored by a kindergarten and nursery school. The parents had each been assigned to choose one of their children who seemed to be going through a period of discouragement. The parent was to plan an activity alone with the discouraged child, carry out the activity, then report on it the following week.

One woman was convinced that her activity had only made things worse. She reported the young child's rebellious public behavior and her determination not to take him out alone again. I asked what the activity had been.

"I was planning a dinner party that night, and I allowed Tommy to go to the grocery store with me," she replied. "All of the other children had to stay home with the sitter, but Tommy got to go all alone with Mommy."

Reflecting back over time spent in a grocery store with my own pre-schoolers, I wondered: What kind of a special time could *that* be? I'm sure the child was aware that, although not competing with his brothers and sisters for attention, he was competing with the artichokes and mushrooms. Not exactly a three-year-old's idea of a good time.

The second disillusioned couple was furious with their unappreciative three-year-old. Their special activity had not been as ordinary an event as a trip to the supermarket. They had included their three-year-old in the observation of a very special religious ceremony (not LDS, in case you're wondering what, short of a temple session, such an activity could be) that was usually attended only by adults. They had taken the child shopping, bought him an expensive new suit, and taken him on a long trip to another part of the state to attend the ceremony, and he had shown his ingratitude by squirming and whining all during the ceremony.

My mind went again to the three-year-olds I had known. To get my kids to try on clothes at that age was like taking them to the dentist. And sitting in church for long periods of time? At least in the grocery store they had the mobility of the cart!

Obviously both sets of parents had made the same mistake. They had failed to consider the needs and wants of the child. A more appropriate activity might have been a trip to the zoo, but the parent with less time or money might have found that, as much as any formal activity, the child would appreciate five minutes of uninterrupted time with Mother watching him build with his blocks. Listening to a primary-grade child read, or watching a budding athlete shoot baskets, can be just as encouraging as an expensive gift of a well-planned family activity. It's the child-centeredness of the time that matters.

Two more ways to teach self-esteem seem to be contradictory at first. One is to provide many success experiences for the child; the other is to allow him the freedom to fail.

The old saying "them that has, gets," certainly applies to success. Most parents understand this instinctively and provide as many success experiences for their children as possible. It isn't a secret that the child who has learned to succeed is willing to work harder for success as he grows older. Remember the way you went all to pieces with joy the first time your baby said "goo," or pulled himself up, or took a step? Then as your child grew older and went out into the world of neighborhood, church, and school, you hoped and prayed that his successes would outnumber his failures. This is as it should be.

But there are times in the growing-up process when a child's achievement will not be successful as measured by adult standards. Are you ever tempted, when doing a crafts project with your children, to say "That's good — but let me just touch it up a little here. . . ." So you touch it up a little here, a little there, until it bears no resemblance to the creative masterpiece your child created? Or when the artist, a little older and more particular, finds that she is unable to complete a task to her liking, what do you do? Do you finish it for her? Do you say, "The materials were cheap, honey; it doesn't matter anyway!"? But it does matter, when the ungainly creation is measured in terms of the amount of time, and concentration, and hopes.

It's hard for a mother to see her child fail at anything, and for many different reasons. Some mothers prefer to feed their young children rather than allow them the freedom to occasionally miss the prescribed goal — the open mouth — with the gooey mess in the weighted dish. Others insist on doing too much for their pre-schoolers; they fear a slight injury or a messy house. It will make a mess! You might get hurt! What will people think? It's got to be pretty! Such are the rationalizations of the overprotective mother.

Children become discouraged when they are not allowed to make mistakes and overcome childhood disasters by themselves. The child who is allowed to take a fall, pick himself up, and then be comforted in an encouraging manner (It really hurts, but it's good to know that you can handle the pain), usually learns to handle fear and pain better than the one who is rushed to, picked up, and pitied. The child who is allowed to make a mess and then encouraged to clean it up usually learns to take care of himself better than the one who grows up in a neat but hands-off environment.

What about praise? Some writers say "Generous praise is essential!" Others say "Praise the act, but not the child." Still others say "Praise is a no-no."

I'm sure it is just a matter of semantics, but I much prefer the word *encouragement* to *praise*. I guess the reason is that, to me, praise implies judgment and manipulation. Many women praise their children (and their husbands) with the hope of a desired result: "You are so big and strong! Just the type I need to carry out the garbage!" It can also be used like a candy bar: "You ate all your Cheerios! You are such a good child! Mommy is so *proud* of you!" Why get their egos all tied up with the garbage and the Cheerios if there are other ways of teaching work and health habits?

I think it is unfair to a child to be judged constantly, to become dependent upon his mother for approval. Isn't it better if we can teach the child to love work, or at least to feel good at having completed a job, whether or not the achievement is rewarded by lavish praise?

I know what you're thinking. Even if you are prepared to admit that there might be some sense in that philosophy, learning not to praise is even harder than learning not to nag! And I agree. By nature, I am one of the most lavish praisers I know. I still can't help saying "That's great!" "I love it!" when one of my kids shows me a completed (or a half-way completed) do-it-yourself project. I mean, you don't just say "Very interesting!" as they do in the books, and get away with it. But I have made some rules for myself, and I think they have influenced at least the flavor of my praise.

First: Don't connect the worth of the child with a deed or accomplishment. For example, I try never to say "You're

such a good girl!'' when my daughter surprises me by cleaning up the kitchen. Why? Because she might think to herself,
''If I *hadn't* cleaned up the kitchen would I be a bad girl?'' I
also try not to use expressions of personal love in connection
with accomplishments. I might say ''I love it when you help
me with the work,'' or ''I love to see the kitchen so clean,''
but I try not to say ''I love you because you are such a good
helper.'' I know that the reason I love her is because she is my
little girl, and I'd love her even if she were a lazy oaf. I want
her to know that my love is unconditional. To balance my
restraint, I often say ''I love you,'' or ''You know, you're a
good kid'' spontaneously, when no accomplishment is involved.

Second: I try never to miss an opportunity to *show appreciation for* or to *rejoice with* my child. When my daughter
cleans the kitchen for me I might say: ''I was so tired, and it
makes me feel so good to have the kitchen cleaned up!'' I'm
telling her how *I* feel, not evaluating her worth. I might
express my appreciation for the same act more than once. A
note of thanks in the child's room when he or she comes home
from school, or even an occasional thank-you note in the
mail, shows that the child's efforts are appreciated. Unless
the child is likely to be teased by his friends, a short note of
thanks in the school snack or the lunch-box might be used
occasionally. Mentioning a helpful act to Dad when he
comes home is another good way to show appreciation.
(''Chad really helped me out this morning. I needed to get the
car out early and he shoveled the driveway so I wouldn't get
stuck!'') This is a new slant on the old ''Wait till your father
gets home!'' routine.

It's easy to find the right words to show appreciation for
services rendered. But what do we do when the child has
accomplished something on his own, not necessarily for us,
but for which he looks to us for approval? We pull out all the
stops and ''rejoice with him.''

The basic difference between the attitude of *rejoicing
with* and *praise* is that in rejoicing with my children I try to let

them know that I am sharing with them the joy that comes from accomplishment or right doing, and not accepting their goodness as a personal favor to me. My goal is to help my children to learn to enjoy creating for the joy of creating, not for the hope of a favorable response from mother and, later, from the teacher, the boss, and/or the public. I want them to learn that there is intrinsic reward in work and in following the Lord's commandments.

This is where it gets sticky. First, my *philosophy* is this: A good thing to say when a child shows you a painting he has done is "I'm so glad you enjoy painting!" I read this suggestion somewhere, and it makes sense. You are not saying "That is beautiful!" because saying "That is beautiful!" may cause problems. First, if it is really not that beautiful the child may know it and he may cross you off his list as a phony. Second, if it really *is* beautiful, and the child knows it, he may have problems when his next painting isn't quite as beautiful. By some aesthetic accident he may have painted himself into a corner, or created a standard that will be difficult to repeat. But if you draw attention to his enjoyment of painting, he may get the idea that mother knows about the thrill that comes with creating and she likes it; so it must be good to feel that way.

But try as I may, I can't just say "I'm so glad you enjoy playing!" when my nine-year-old completes a pass for the winning touchdown of his Pony League Game; and I can't just say "I'm so glad you enjoy dancing!" when my daughter is the most beautiful Sugar Plum Fairy in the Christmas program. I let my joy be felt through the look on my face and a hearty hug. (Okay, I'll admit a few "that was super!"'s escape.) But I try to remember to call attention to the feeling inside ("Isn't it a great feeling!") and not to the pride they have bestowed upon the family. Why? Because if my son should ever happen to fumble the ball at a strategic moment, or if my daughter should happen to fall on her face in the middle of a pirouette, I don't want him or her to think that that has shamed the family.

But what about the really important things, like morality and honor? I have heard many stories about people who have found themselves in difficult positions and later confessed that they were able to resist temptation because they knew that if they gave in it would hurt their parents. I will admit that I have stayed on the straight and narrow often for the same reason. If I wanted to prove a point, I might argue that it would be better for the youth to be able to say "I resisted temptation because, in light of the consequences, I knew it was the right thing to do"; or, "I resisted temptation because I knew the Lord would want me to." But let's be honest — resisting temptation is resisting temptation, and whatever the motivation, I can't knock it! I believe that we as parents exert an influence on our children without consciously saying "Do this or that for me." I believe that the child who loves and respects his parents feels a need to make them proud of him *without* the parents having to capitalize on this need for approval. I believe that as we help children to develop as individuals we do not estrange them from us but rather give them the tools to better control themselves in any situation. They are *naturally* dependent upon us; our job is to help them grow in ability to depend upon themselves for approval and acceptance.

There are others besides ourselves and our families who need encouragement, who need to be reminded that they are important and worthy. This is a difficult time for women in the Church. Because times are changing and problems are developing in complexity, it no longer suffices if we tend to "the poor, sick, needy, and afflicted" and the "widows and orphans" in the traditional ways. The problem might be that the divorcee in the ward is sick and tired of being looked upon as "The Divorcee in the Ward," or that the needy need a little honest encouragement more than a casserole and a salad.

The time has come when we need to discard labels and accept our sisters unconditionally as we accept our children. "She's a *working* mother!" "She leans a little toward the

counter-culture — not exactly the clean-cut Mormon type.''
''I'm sorry, I just don't have anything in common with Sister
Hoffman — she's too Suzy Homemaker for me!'' We all
have doubts, and we are all in desperate need of someone, at
some time, to help us to keep above the horrid state of
self-depreciation.

There are people outside the boundaries of the Church
who could use some love and attention, too. Billions of them!
There's so much to be done, and in only twenty-four hours a
day. Where do I start, and is it all right to wait until I get it all
together myself before I start helping a sister? Sometimes I
feel so helpless, so unable to determine my priorities. Then
the words come back, prodding me, lifting me up:

> I am only one,
> But I *am* one. . . .

Chapter 3

Honor the Priesthood: Potent or Potential

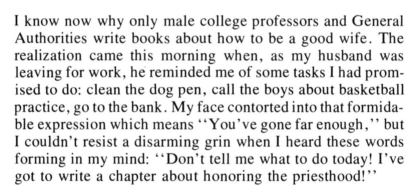

I know now why only male college professors and General Authorities write books about how to be a good wife. The realization came this morning when, as my husband was leaving for work, he reminded me of some tasks I had promised to do: clean the dog pen, call the boys about basketball practice, go to the bank. My face contorted into that formidable expression which means "You've gone far enough," but I couldn't resist a disarming grin when I heard these words forming in my mind: "Don't tell me what to do today! I've got to write a chapter about honoring the priesthood!"

The realization came again as I sat down at the typewriter. For years I have been formulating this book in my mind: a communication that might allow me to share some encouragement with women like myself. Subconsciously I've tucked little experiences and insights into that portion of my mind headed "Church Women." Consciously I have written little notes and put them somewhere or other for safe keeping. But the subconscious messages to "remember this" and the notes to myself were for some distant time when I was wise and oh, so very righteous! Today I am wondering, Is it presumptuous for me to claim understanding of so celestial a principle as honoring the priesthood?

So I must be honest and admit that today I am not the sage and saintly writer I had planned to be. In all probability I don't understand this principle completely. If I did, I probably wouldn't make faces and think ungracious mumblings every time my husband repeated the list of errands for the day. If I did I wouldn't grit my teeth every time he handled the children in a way that didn't quite agree with my carefully researched and definitely prejudiced ideas of child-rearing. On the other hand, it is because I have struggled with this principle, while recognizing it to be *the* most important item on my own personal earthly lesson plan, that I feel a need to talk about it in an over-the-kitchen-table and not an over-the-pulpit way.

First, let me introduce myselves to you. There are two of me. The first one grew up organizing clubs so that she could be president, and creating little newspapers so that she could be editor. She organized neighborhood story-hours so that she could be storyteller and produced plays so that she could be Star. "She's got qualities of leadership," the grown-ups used to say. I think they meant "She's a bossy little snip!"

When the little leader grew up, she went to college. "To get a husband," they joked, but she knew it was to get a degree. She wanted to be a teacher. No, not just a teacher. She wanted to be the kind they asked to do displays at state conventions and then maybe work at a demonstration school, or get her name in an education journal, or become a supervisor! Unless, of course, she were blessed with a family of her own. . . .

The second me grew up wanting, above everything, a temple marriage. She played dress-ups, dolls, and even kind-and-pleasant waitress, and thus prepared herself to be beautiful and submissive. She dreamed of the day when a worthy young man would place her on a pedestal and carry her to the temple, there to begin a life of unity and bliss forever. When she grew older she attended all her meetings, and especially M.I.A. standards nights, where she heard beautiful young brides describe a life of joy spent in caring for an adoring husband and planning for an infinite number of children. She accompanied the little leader to college, hoping quietly that in addition to getting the degree the little leader would run across an ambitious, worshipful, adoring young returned missionary like the ones described at the standards nights, and would then disappear into the sunset while the second me, beautifully and submissively, took care of the home and the children.

The two me's coexisted peacefully and happily, and our dreams came true. But some time after the temple ceremony the sweet and submissive me was confronted by two horrible realities: First, the missionary she had chosen had somehow developed into a human being, with a real personality, not at all like the worshipful prince in the story. And, horror of horrors, the little leader, try as she might to remain buried under the delicate bridal bouquet, kept coming back to life! Without these two disasters, the little homemaker reflected wistfully, life would have been beautiful and serene. But she felt helpless to deal with the two strong-minded characters who threatened to rob her of her tranquility.

Now, sixteen years later, it is the sweet, submissive me who lies peacefully under the somewhat flaky bouquet of blue and white carnations, while the little leader is struggling to find the serenity that comes with the art of submission. The struggle has been and still is difficult, and the young, ambitious returned missionary bears some scars of battle, too. The temple marriage, instead of casting a magic spell of love and beauty, as my idealistic counterpart had supposed, has served as a reminder of the solemnity of the commitment. The little leader reflects on the depth of wisdom and compassion she has gained as a result of her close association with the kind and brilliant husband who has not yet mastered the art of wife-worship.

How do you dissolve a myth without shattering it? How can I build on truth without appearing to destroy a beautiful dream? For I fear that false expectations have, at times, led me in the wrong direction and caused me to waste some time in my quest for self-mastery.

Probably the reason why there is so much misunderstanding about honoring the priesthood is that it is all mixed up with that man-woman mystique. Even in the Church one sometimes wonders whether there isn't a constant power-struggle going on between the sexes. Look at this purely Mormon adage, for example: "The husband is the head of the house, but the wife is the neck that turns the head." This seems to imply that some gentle manipulation is going on, making the husband look little more prestigious than a controlled politician.

Especially today, with the "Lo-heres! Lo-theres!" of feminism vs. anti-feminism, I believe that it is necessary for a woman to come to grips with her "womanism" before she can honestly honor the priesthood in her home. There is more to "honoring" than simply submitting to, and the woman who is resentfully playing a role with which she is uncomfortable may be dulling her natural ability to honor (which means to esteem, respect, and/or adore). It is hard to respect, let alone adore, a man you regard as your warden.

The patriarchal order is of God. I know that, and because I know it I can no more deny it than the Three Witnesses could deny their testimony of the Book of Mormon. It is an eternal truth that a woman must learn to obey, support, honor, and assist her husband in order to merit the blessings of celestial marriage and eternal progression. It is true that worthy women have been promised the privilege of ruling over kingdoms with their husbands. These truths are written in the scriptures and established in the writings of the prophets.

But how open to personal interpretation such generalities can become! For example, some men quote "the husband is the head of the wife" (Ephesians 5:23) and regard the marriage license as permission to control, coerce, and use. I know of husbands who have denied permission for their wives to finish high school, to vote, or to have contact with friends and relatives because they feel it is one of their "rights" to deny such permission. On the other hand, I know of wives who have taken advantage of the admonition to "provoke [their husbands] to righteousness" and nagged relentlessly with a clear conscience.

Other wives are aware of the admonition to "obey [their] husbands in righteousness" and follow it to the letter. The trouble is, their husbands hardly ever ask them to do anything in righteousness, so they never have to obey. How righteous does the righteousness have to be in order to merit obedience? If your husband tells you not to spend any money, but you need a year's supply of food, isn't it permissible to override his unrighteous commandment? You see, it is easy to find loopholes in the letter of the law. We need the spirit of the law to help us.

Submitting to anyone is difficult, and especially difficult to the woman with a strong sense of self-direction. In the Church and in a democracy, freedom and free agency are valued highly. "How much of my own self-direction should I maintain? How much should I relinquish?" It is difficult to know the answers. In my early days of marriage I went back and forth between being a dull piece of modeling clay and an insistent maintainer-of-rights. Submission cannot be forced; neither can it be feigned for very long. As in every other principle of the gospel, the right way to submit is *powerfully!*

As yet, I have found it impossible to completely submit to another human being, even one so strong and good as my husband. But I think I've found a starting point.

I am learning to submit to the will of my Father in heaven, and I know that through this submission I will eventually learn to submit to my husband. I have had just enough experience with my Father in heaven to know that submission to him doesn't involve any of the risks that we take when we submit ourselves to another human being. For example:

1. *You never have to worry about how far to submit.* With your Father in heaven you *know*! You submit completely. Webster's definition of submit is "to yield, resign, or surrender to power, will, or authority." Make that power, will, *and* authority.

2. *You don't have to worry about losing your individuality.* Our Father in heaven, omniscient being that he is, would not stoop to such a human trick as to try to pour one of his original creations into someone else's mold.

3. *You don't have to worry about becoming an uninteresting yes-person.* When I am really "in" with my Father in heaven, I am more gorgeous, creative, self-directed, and energetic than when I'm not.

4. *You don't need to worry about giving up more than you'll get.* When you submit yourself to the will of our Heavenly Father he usually slips in a few blessings you didn't even know you needed: opportunities, those mini-miracles that make the day go easier, abilities you didn't know you had. There's no way you can come out on the short end.

When you submit yourself to the will of your Heavenly Father you find yourself becoming the kind of wife you know you should be. You're more generous, flexible, and loving, partly because in becoming aligned with the forces of good you become a stockholder in the eternal reservoir of love, and partly because you are more likely to feel good about yourself and are therefore able to become less defensive and give more of yourself. But it's more fun than you thought it would be: You don't think of yourself as the woman in the laundry detergent commercial that you always feared you'd become when you established yourself as a loving and devoted homemaker!

Another advantage that comes from heavenly direction is the reduced need for the judgmental attitudes that we seem to rely on in our human state. It is not uncommon for the wife of a nonmember or an inactive Mormon to shut out the admonition to honor the priesthood in her home, rationalizing that her husband doesn't hold the priesthood, or that he doesn't honor his *own* priesthood so there is nothing there to honor. It is my understanding that all husbands and fathers should be accorded the same love and respect to which a priesthood holder is entitled. True, a non-priesthood-holding father may not be allowed to participate in Church ordinances, but by virtue of his position in the family his authority to guide and direct the family should never be usurped by another family member or by a priesthood holder outside the home.

Sometimes a woman becomes frustrated because she feels that she and her husband are working at cross purposes, and she feels it necessary to shield her children from what she thinks is a bad influence. It's easy to put down a husband with unacceptable habits, both to friends and to children: "Daddy knows he shouldn't smoke, he's just too weak to stop"; or, "I can't make it to my meeting; Fred makes it so hard for me to live the gospel!" This is violating one of the rules I have discovered for honoring the priesthood (or prevention of cruelty to husbands). The rule is: *Help him to look good.*

In terms of amount of time spent in discussion, the subject of husbands' shortcomings is a close contender to gossip in some women's circles. The traditional complaints are still with us: He works too much; he doesn't work hard enough. He doesn't spend enough time with the family; he never lets me do anything by myself. He spends too much time at church; he's not religious enough. He's overprotective; he expects me to do too much. Lately new ones have been added: He's chauvinistic; he won't share in the household responsibilities. The advertising industry has even begun using films of women shaming their husbands for using the wrong product to clean the floor!

Quite possibly, women's complaints are well founded and not just hearsay. Then what's wrong with a little honest complaining among friends? It probably doesn't hurt the husband that much; after all, in such a conversation "the husband" usually becomes a faceless opponent, and no one will ever remember which complaint goes with which husband when the conversation is over. The damage, then, has to be to some mysterious network of feelings and action inside the complaining wife, and eventually to her relationship with the complained-about husband.

Much more damage is done when put-downs come from the wife to the children. I was impressed with the observation made by a prominent woman lecturer that "Mother has the power to make even a real loser look like a king in the eyes of his children." She also has the power to make a fine man look like a tramp.

A seminary teacher once related this incident to me. The class had been discussing the importance of attending meetings. A young man who had recently joined the Church asked this question: "My Dad is not a member of the Church. He goes to school at nights, and Tuesday is his only week night at home. On Tuesdays he likes me to help him in the yard or to work on his antique car. Tuesday is Aaronic Priesthood activities night and my priests' leader is always urging me to attend. I feel as if I'm caught in the middle! Should I refuse to help my Dad?"

This is typical of the kind of mind-boggling questions which come up when members of a family do not have the same priorities. Even though it didn't help her attempt to reach her lesson objective, the seminary teacher was prompted to answer that when two laws are in conflict it is advisable to choose the higher law. "Honor thy father and thy mother" is one of the Ten Commandments, and for the boy to obey his father seemed to be, in this case, following the higher law.

It would be impossible for me to make a list of priorities of laws. I do know that living the patriarchal order and honoring husband and father is near the top. When in doubt, check with your Father in heaven. He knows for sure.

I have only one more rule for wives wishing to improve their relationship with their husbands. It is: *Live the Golden Rule – Somewhat Modified.*

The Golden Rule is "Do unto others as you would have them do unto you." The modified Golden Rule is "Do unto others as *they* would like to be done unto." In other words, consider your husbands needs, his likes and dislikes, his wishes. Show a real concern for him, uncommon individual that he may be, rather than bowing to your own desires or to outward appearances. I know a woman who gave her husband a shovel every Father's Day until he got the hint that he should be working in the yard more. That is an example of *not* keeping the modified Golden Rule. This is another one:

My husband and I were married in December. His birthday is in January. The first year we were married we were somewhat strapped financially; he was still in school, and a large portion of my teaching salary went to pay for encyclopedias and china I had purchased before we met. After Christmas and a big wedding reception, we were broke.

I wanted to do something special (and free) for his birthday. I couldn't cook a gourmet meal — we were both sick of the venison I had frozen for special occasions. I didn't know how to knit or sew. Then it came to me — I would share with him my literary gifts!

When his birthday arrived, I got up before dawn and wrote little bits of poetry which I hid in his wallet and his key case and tied to his toothbrush and razor. I was proud of my jingles — I felt like a twentieth-century Elizabeth Barrett Browning, only with a sense of humor. A note in the shoe, another in the underwear drawer. I was excited in awaiting his response.

The day came and went without one peal of laughter from behind the closed bathroom door and without one shout of glee as he opened his attaché case. He didn't even remember to say thanks. I was crushed and disappointed. What a shame to waste such creative talent on an unappreciative recipient!

Looking back, I can see what happened. My husband, I know now, is a goal-directed person. He doesn't even read the funnies! Reading little jingles, albeit inspired, in the bathroom on a close time schedule is not his idea of a happy birthday. *My* goal had not been to please him so much as to receive his praise and adoration for my cleverness. So now, when his birthday arrives and I am still suffering the financial results of a before-Christmas spending spree, I write him a note promising him a complete, non-interrupted TV football game the next time he desires to watch one, with homemade pink popcorn and all the soda pop he wants me to serve him. He loves it.

As with gaining any positive self-concept, there is a circular aspect to learning to honor the priesthood. One success makes the next one easier, and it doesn't matter where you begin. You can start by behaving in a more thoughtful and loving manner, and thus increase the spirituality in your home; or you can start by increasing your own spirituality, and thus increase your capacity for love and thoughtfulness. You can increase your own self-confidence, and thus increase your capacity for consideration of another; or you can reap the positive results of an improved marriage relationship brought about by your own change in behavior and thus increase your self-confidence.

Honoring the priesthood is a lifestyle. It includes being at peace with yourself, being in tune with the Lord, and being willing to make the first move as often as is necessary to show acceptance of and appreciation for the man at the head of your family. There are hundreds of ways to show love for your husband and thus set an example of honor and respect in your home. I have no lists to share and no easy answers. Your solutions will have more meaning both to you and to your family if you create them yourself than if you read and implement them recipe-book fashion.

Chapter 4

The Art of Being First Counselor

I've been president of a Church auxiliary organization, and I don't really enjoy administrative responsibilities. I've been Sunday School secretary, and just the thought of making reports gives me the jitters. I've even been M.I.A. Sports Director — me, the little girl who always hid in the dressing room when her junior high gym class played softball! I'm a lifetime Church member, and my husband and I have moved a lot, so I've held just about every position open to women in the Church. But by far the most difficult position I've ever held is that of counselor in a presidency.

It's unfortunate, feeling as I do about being a counselor, that I keep ending up in that position. Okay, I'll admit — it's not an unfortunate coincidence. No more than it's coincidental that my fourth grader is required to spend more time on language than on math. It figures. Language is his most difficult subject.

I can remember how thrilled I was with the principle of ''programmed learning'' when it was presented to me by one of my religion professors at Brigham Young University. He explained that each of us has certain lessons we have to learn in life, or certain traits we must acquire. We are given an opportunity to learn a lesson, and if we learn it we don't have to endure any more trials or experiences designed to teach that specific lesson. It sounded so simple, and I decided then, in my senior year, that I would use my insight and save myself a lot of unnecessary trials and problems; that each time I found myself in a difficult situation I would find the basic lesson to be taught, learn the lesson, order my life accordingly, and save myself a lot of re-trials. It made sense.

It still makes sense. But experience has taught me what a religion class could not: that the mind is a better student than the emotions, and that until knowing and doing are on the same level, the skill isn't considered mastered. There are no multiple-choice or true-false tests where eternal principles are involved; only tests of performance.

I used to ask myself: "Why must I learn the art of counselorship, anyway? Isn't it more important to be a good teacher?" Then one evening, as I sat in our meetinghouse enjoying a presentation by one of the Education Week instructors, the bomb was dropped. The light came on. "I can best compare the role of the wife," the learned messenger announced, "to that of a counselor in a presidency." Suddenly I realized why the Lord was so determined to teach me to be a good counselor.

In analyzing why it is difficult for me to be a good counselor in a Primary or Relief Society presidency, I am able to see more clearly the reasons why I sometimes have problems adjusting to the "wife" role. First, the basic job description. In the present Church organization each position in a presidency has certain responsibilities attached to it. The counselor is accountable for all the programs which fall under her jurisdiction, as well as for any extra assignments the president wishes to give her. Some of the responsibilities are enjoyable, others may be tedious, but they're clearly defined. Cut and dried. Open and shut. Simple Simon.

Hold on! I've found a good many discrepancies between *my* interpretation of the job description handed out for the first counselor to the patriarch of the Virginia Branch of the Day family and the interpretation of said patriarch. To me, "keep house" means to maintain sanitary conditions acceptable to the Fairfax County Board of Health: No dirt or germs allowed, but a little clutter is acceptable. My husband got the idea somewhere that home should be a haven from the outside world, and a haven to him is neat and oh, so very well organized! And try as I might, I can't remember anything in the marriage ceremony about making phone calls and running errands. But these tasks are, I am finding, undeniably stated in my unwritten job description.

There have been times in my life when I have been downright rebellious about my job description; unreasonably so. I have felt that in bowing to my husband's demands for a neat, well-organized home I would be giving up some autonomy, some individuality. I believe there have been times when I have unconsciously but purposely left a floor unswept or dishes in the sink as a distorted symbol of victory. I have groaned about assignments and carried a suit around in my car for weeks instead of dropping it off at the cleaners' as instructed. The rules for my when-I'm-good-and-ready games would make chess look simple. Are there any games that you have invented to complicate the carrying-out of your home responsibilities?

When my youngest child started school I began thinking about trying to find a part-time job that I could work at while the children were gone. I got a little panicky when I started to write my resumé. My educational background looked okay, and I knew I had pretty good references up until (had it been *that* long?) nine years ago. Though the past nine years had been full ones for me, they looked rather barren on a "record of past employment." I frantically tried to think of people I had known professionally during the past nine years who would verify that I was still able-bodied and of sound mind.

The thought came to me, "What if I were to ask my husband for a letter of reference?" I was horrified at the picture of the kind of check-list employers are sometimes asked to fill out, and how my husband would have to answer the questions if he were honest. After a busy week, it might look something like this:

Work habits: (*Oh, why, oh, why do they put that one first?*) Sloppy.

Ability to follow directions: (*But I don't WANT a job following DIRECTIONS!*) Poor.

Initiative: (*Now, you CAN'T say I lack initiative . . .*) She'll do anything, as long as it's her own idea.

Is applicant well-informed regarding her specific field of service? (*Gotcha on that one!*) She's read all the books on child development and gourmet cooking. But it's been weeks since she's discussed world affairs with me, and I don't think she has any idea what I'm doing, although I've suggested several books and articles about my field of labor that she might read. I'll give her a yes and no on that one, since being a wife isn't exactly a *specific* field of service.

Efficiency: Every day she outlines her work carefully. In fact, she could probably do the ironing in the time it takes her to outline her work!

Flexibility: Excellent, unless I should ask her to change her plans.

Punctuality: Improving slowly.

Dependability: She's extremely dependable in Church and civic duties, but I'm still waiting for that button to be sewn on my favorite jacket.

Creativity: Check-plus. Except for the fried hamburger and carrot sticks we've had for supper for the last week or so.

Sense of humor: Excellent. Unless the laugh's on her.

Well, forget that idea. I'll just have to find an employer who will believe I've been suspended in time for nine years!

Although it is possibly the most time-consuming part, the pre-determined job description is not the most important part of a counselor's calling. I was reminded forcefully in a setting-apart blessing that a counselor's most important function is to help and support the president in any way she can. I have been reminded *twice* in blessings that the counselor is to assist, counsel with, and give ideas to the president, but that in the end the president is to make the final decision and the counselors should then support her unquestioningly.

Learning to be helpful and supportive to an auxiliary president has helped me to be more helpful and supportive as a wife. I have learned some things about organizations that also apply to homes.

As I grow in years and experience I find that the "hows" and "whats" become less important and the "whys" and "whos" become more vital. For instance, I used to think that the way to be a profitable servant was to have the best roadshow, the most reverent Primary, or the most elegant Relief Society luncheon. I thought, I prayed, I planned. The end result was the important thing, and those people who proved to be agreeable, dependable, and helpful in the project felt well rewarded. Those who were unwilling or undependable made me feel depressed or threatened, but they were, as adversaries, overcome. The Show Went On, and I was rewarded by the roar of the crowd, the compliments of the guests, or the praise of the stake board.

Now, I still feel that excellence is a goal worth striving for, but I know that the reason for all the programs of the Church is to foster the growth of the members, and I feel a great responsibility to conduct all Church business in a manner that will help others to build their self-esteem rather than lower it. I have found that, in a presidency, a feeling of unity and love will have a more far-reaching effect on an organization than all the clever ideas, effective lessons, and breathtaking programs we could ever put together. I have learned to keep quiet and relax when it might be easier to argue or push a point. *I am working on* the ability to maintain a pleasant approach when the thing to do is so obviously to complain, blame someone, or give up.

If I can put the organization before myself in a presidency, should I be able to put the peace and love of a family before myself at home? I should, but for every ounce of self-control it takes to behave agreeably in a Church meeting it takes a pound to help me to act in a far-sighted and selfless way at home. I have reached the point at which I can be somewhat objective about my ward; after all, I only spend a few hours a week at church, and I can afford to compromise on things. But my whole life revolves around my home; there is so much at stake there. Maybe, too, it is the awesomeness of my home responsibilities that makes me feel uptight at times. If I make a mistake at Relief Society it may make me look bad, but there is always someone else who can take over and make things right. But if I fail as wife and mother, I've really *failed*.

Probably the reasons that make being a first counselor to my husband more difficult than being first counselor to a president are the very reasons why I'm so determined to succeed. My mind knows what to do, now, and just what direction I should take. Give me another ninety years, and I may be able to educate my emotions!

Chapter 5

Constructive Coexistence

◇○◁━━━━━━━━━━━━━━━━━━━━━━━━━━━

Linguists assume that just because a group of people uses the same words to describe the same symbols, its members are able to communicate. Families know better.

In our family, for example, when my husband says "Do we have any ice cream?" an inexperienced observer might think he was asking a question. I know the truth; he is giving a command, or making a request. My mind quickly translates the words from English to Day-ese, and I hear "Get me some ice cream, please." And anyone who heard my son Brad come in from school and say angrily "Steve Anderson is the worst smart alec in school!" might think he was simply sharing his opinion of a boy at school; but I would know he was saying "I had a bad day, Mom, and I need to talk about it."

The term *communicate* has become a household word; but unfortunately, for most of us it hasn't as yet become a household habit. For years I used to complain to my husband, "We never talk!" because we didn't have regular heart-to-heart philosophical discussions as I thought married people were supposed to. "Okay," he'd say, "talk!" Then, completely out of keeping with my character, I'd find myself speechless. What should I talk *about?* When I finally learned the real meaning of communication I got the message. Walt Disney's "Thumper" had been told by his father "If you can't say something nice, don't say nothing at all!" My husband believed talking was only for when there was something to say.

In marriage, communication isn't just an inspiring exchange of words. A wife who never receives the consideration she feels she deserves, a husband who feels nagged at and imposed upon, the "I try so hard, and what does it get me?" syndrome — these are all results of poor communication. Real communication results more from a high quality of listening than from a large quantity of talking. Real communication can pave the way to the accomplishment of individual and mutual goals.

Speaking of individual goals, a woman has several options in her attempt to have things go her way. She can insist, beg, cry, or pout. She can also threaten, trick, flatter, or play helpless. All of these usually get results; however, these methods all have one feature in common. They presume that one member of the contest is strong and one is weak (or one is smart and one is stupid). They do not contain the elements of mutual trust that are necessary to build the honest kind of communication that can form the basis of a long-term love relationship.

I have found four steps to arriving at a truly workable relationship. They are:

(1) Avoid being defensive.
(2) Express your feelings.
(3) Encourage your husband to express his feelings.
(4) Bargain for mutual profit.

Avoid being defensive. The scene takes place in your dining room. It's family night, and you have gone to special pains, as you always do on Monday, to prepare a special dinner. But you got into a traffic jam on the way home from visiting teaching and didn't get home to turn down the oven heat as you had intended to. Your husband, who likes rare, juicy meat, comments on the cuisine:

"The roast is burned."

A simple statement of fact. He may have said it thinking you didn't *know* the roast was burned, or he may have felt a need to see whether his vocal cords were still working. *I* don't know why husbands say things like that! But many of them do, and the important thing is your response.

Most women don't hear a simple statement of fact. They don't even hear "The roast is burned." They hear "You are a bad cook." "We've been married all these years and you still can't cook a piece of meat the way I like it!" "You have just made a charred waste out of $7.50!"

The day you can hear "The roast is burned" as a simple statement of fact will be the day your communication improves by a tremendous percentage. It will mean that you have trained your ears and your mind (your heart, if you want to be sentimental about it) to be rational, and it is only a short step from rational to warm, and understanding, and all those other things that wives are supposed to be.

It may not be burned roasts that cause you to be defensive. Determine what it is. You might even list the things your husband says or does that make you feel that you have to retaliate and remind him that *he's* not exactly the twentieth century's answer to Sir Lancelot, or that start you sorting through your list of excuses to justify yourself. Perhaps it's a remark like "What's this check for fifty dollars made out to Cash?"; or, "I thought you went to a Primary meeting *last* week!"; or "I liked your hair better long."

For as long as it takes to change your reaction, be conscious of what remarks or questions cause you to feel that you have to defend yourself, then try to respond in a nondefensive way. If you find yourself feeling uptight and angry even when you have responded rationally, go on to Step 2 and learn to express your feelings.

Express your feelings. Traditionally women have reacted to a lack of consideration in two ways: gunnysacking and attacking.

Imagine this situation: Ever since you moved into your house five years ago you have dreamed of redecorating the living room. You have planned the color scheme, even chosen the wallpaper and the drapery material. Your husband has hinted that a large tax refund will be forthcoming this year, and in your mind there is a possibility that you can use the refund money to begin redecorating. But the tax refund arrives without your knowing it, and your husband surprises the family with the expensive pool table he has been wanting.

You are terribly disappointed. Not only had you hoped for the money to use yourself, but you hate pool. The huge pool table makes your family room look small and crowded. But you know that a wife should be goodnatured and supportive so you pretend to be happy and excited. After all, it was his money to begin with.

Or maybe you don't respond in that way. "It's better," you rationalize, "to let him know how I feel." You might cry or shout, or say something like: "You inconsiderate rat! You *promised* me I could have that money for the living room! I *hate* that ugly green thing; it makes our house look like the local hangout!"

Let's examine each response. The first one, sacrificing your own desires graciously, fits into the acceptable model of the supportive wife, doesn't it? And it would provide a nice solution if the story were to end there. But does it?

The trouble with pretending is that the act may be covering up feelings of anger, disappointment, and hostility without providing any kind of outlet. We call this "gunnysacking," with the implication that you put all your negative feelings in a gunnysack and try to ignore them. The problem is that even big gunnysacks fill up sooner or later, and when they are holding enough repressed feelings something has to give. The real feelings may burst forth in the next argument (in which case you've completely blown it as far as your future as an actress is concerned), or they may come out subtly as you begin making bitter remarks about the pool table, your ugly old living room, or your husband. Or they may continue to stay repressed for years until, added to other unexpressed hurts and disappointments, they add up to a psychosomatic ailment, a nervous breakdown, or a violent temper tantrum.

Does that mean that it's better to attack, as in the second example? It may be better for your own health, but the *relationship* won't especially flourish in the presence of name-calling and accusations. Then *what*, for goodness' sake?

One way to allow yourself freedom of expression without hurting your relationship with another person is to simply and honestly express your feelings. "Honey, I'm disappointed. I had really counted on that money to redecorate the living room. I guess that's why I didn't act that excited when you brought in the pool table." Now he knows how you feel, and he will probably be more considerate next time. You've expressed your feelings and will probably feel better inside, and you haven't said anything bitter or ugly. If *disappointed* is too mild a word to express your true feelings, tell it like it is. Furious? Shattered? Sick? But keep it on the level of your feelings.

Timing is important when you share your feelings. It will be most effective if you can respond honestly immediately, if this can be done without causing additional problems. Although some authorities on family relationships suggest that it is sometimes good to have an objective third party to observe a confrontation, the time to open up is not in front of a group of friends or family members, nor when your husband is rushing to keep an appointment.

But neither is six months later the right time to respond to an event! Let's go back to the pool table episode. Let's imagine that when you realize that your husband has spent the tax refund for a pool table you feel upset, disappointed, and sick. If you feel *so* upset, disappointed, and sick that you feel you can't live with the purchase, the time to mention it might be immediately, before the thing is unpacked. But if you see how excited the family is and decide that you can live with the pool table but still want to express your feelings, the time might be later that night when you are alone with your husband.

Moreover, if you decide you can live with the pool table, don't wait until months later when your husband has purchased a new fishing rod instead of redecorating the living room and then decide to say "And furthermore, about that pool table you brought home last April. . . ." Expressing feelings can be harmful if it is done retroactively, especially when the stored-up hurts and disappointments come tumbling out in rapid succession. Generally speaking, it is best to discuss only current events. (I don't mean only those you read about in the newspaper!)

It is also important to try to determine your *primary emotion* when you attempt to express your feelings. "Angry" is a common catchall, but it is usually not the first emotion you feel. You may be angry when your husband criticizes the burned roast, but you are probably angry because he has made you feel *inadequate*. You may be angry when he forgets to call you to tell you he will be a little late on a snowy night, but you are probably angry because he has caused you to be *worried*. You may feel angry when he forgets your birthday, but the anger may stem from the fact that you feel *unloved* or *unappreciated*. A husband may be able to do some things to help you feel more adequate, more loved and appreciated, and less worried, but he is bound to feel frustrated and, well, *angry*, when all he is confronted with is anger! Although anger is a perfectly acceptable and expressible emotion, try to look behind the anger to determine whether there is another more basic emotion bothering you.

You must constantly remind yourself to express only feelings, or emotions. It is amazing how creative we are at finding ways to get our digs in. Don't fall into the trap of thinking that just because you start out with "I feel . . ." you are safe. You haven't got the right idea if you can't resist the impulse to say, "I feel . . . that you are an inconsiderate, intolerant, undependable oaf!"

The circle of communication is only partially completed when you learn to express your own feelings. The feeling of closeness and non-competitiveness really begins to come through when you learn to *listen to your husband's feelings*. This may prove to be more difficult than it appears, because although husbands are extremely open and honest in many ways (such as giving accurate descriptions of burnt roasts and runs in stockings) not many of them are adept at expressing their own emotions.

Obviously, telling your husband to talk to you is not the way to get him to share his feelings. There are hundreds of things we can do to change our method of communication without *telling* our husbands anything. The first thing we must do is to convince ourselves that we are interested in determining how our husbands feel.

There have been many, *many* books and articles written on the subject of listening. It has come to our attention that as a people we have lost the ability to listen to others. I first became acquainted with this idea when I was in graduate school. My first reaction was that this problem didn't apply to me, but that I'd give it the test anyway. At school I noticed that as I stood in the hall talking with a group of friends I'd listen just well enough so that I could say "Uh-huh" or

"Oh, no!," or express my opinion at just the right time, but my eyes were searching the halls for someone to say "Hi" to who was not in the group. I noticed it again a few years later when I would occasionally gather for lunch or just a chat with a group of young mothers. It seemed that we were all vying for a chance to talk, looking for a break in the conversation, watching for "our turn." Later, when I was truly trying to help a friend who wanted to confide in me, I realized that instead of really hearing what she was saying I was worrying about what I would say to her.

Listening means more than keeping quiet and letting someone else talk, although that is a very good beginning. It's a real accomplishment to keep your mind on what is being said, whether it's a talk in sacrament meeting, instructions, an anecdote, or a pouring out of confidences. It's important to listen *appropriately*, too — there is nothing more irritating than to be corrected on an inconsequential detail as you approach the punchline of a story, or nothing more infuriating than to have someone attempt to help you "explore your feelings" when you are explaining how to get from the state capitol to the fairgrounds.

But, for those times when it *is* appropriate to listen for feelings, here's how. The first few rules are simple. Listen. Listen. Listen. Consciously.

After you have learned to listen, you can begin to ask yourself: "How is he feeling when he says these things? Is he expressing joy? anger? frustration?" Your response can indicate that you are interested in his feelings and that you respect his right to feel them, even if they're not always the ones you would like him to feel. For instance, you may understand "lonely," "misunderstood," or "unsure of myself," but you must also be prepared to deal with "hassled," "pressured," and "crowded." In adopting a "listening for feelings" attitude we will educate ourselves to feel less of a need to defend our own weaknesses and more of a desire to provide for the needs of our husbands.

I think the greatest advantage in a really communicative marriage is that it plays down the old cat-and-mouse, Dagwood-and-Blondie type of relationship where one is in control and the other is a general flunkie, or one is the winner and one is the loser. Still, marriage is a difficult relationship in that as long as there are two people sharing a house, a room, an income, and a child (or children), there will be times when goals conflict. Even if you and your husband are fortunate enough to have religious and moral views in common, there are as many possibilities for divergent goals and beliefs as there are facets of your personalities.

"Bargaining for mutual profit" sounds like something that goes on in a labor union, but in actuality it can be a very practical tool for husbands and wives who occasionally find themselves in a deadlock situation.

The advice to put the needs of the other first is beautiful and practical. But we're human, and not all of us can invariably follow that advice completely at our present stage of development. There should be allowances for needs that are just too important to be compromised; a way in which we can disagree without being disagreeable.

Prerequisites for admission to the bargaining table are the ability to respond in a nondefensive manner (at least more than half the time) and the ability to express and respond to feelings. If these skills haven't been mastered, bargaining can be just another way to gain power or a glorified manipulative device. So before the bargaining begins, both parties must have a basis of trust that they will not be taken advantage of.

We are all committed to certain ideals and principles; but we are more strongly committed to some than to others. There are some which are so much a part of us that to compromise them would be to destroy ourselves. Then there are some which are extremely important to us, but which we could compromise if it were absolutely necessary. There are some, lower on the hierarchy, which we would hate to give up but could if we had to, and still others which we find convenient but not important. The key is to compromise on the less important ones willingly, then try to strike a workable agreement so that each of you can reach those personal goals which are of primary importance.

Here's a hypothetical situation. Your husband just isn't excited about having family night. You can't really feel that you have done your part as a mother unless your family has a regular family night; in fact, this has been bothering you a lot lately. You've tried planning and carrying out a family night by yourself, but you've found that your husband is offended by your taking the initiative, and there is a worse feeling in your home as a result of your attempts. You're trapped.

This is a case for the bargaining table. *If* you have been accepting of your husband and haven't tried to change him recently, there is a good possibility that you will be able to strike a bargain that will prove advantageous to both of you. First you express your feelings. You *do* tell him that you feel uptight, worried, and uncomfortable about not having family night, because by expressing your own personal feelings you are not trying to make him feel like a neglectful ogre. You do *not* argue that the President of the Church has stated that every family should have family night, and that if your children go down the road of sin it will be their father's fault for neglecting his patriarchal duty.

You then suggest that because family night is so important to you, and because you know Monday night football is important to him, you are willing to make some adjustments of your own to make his life more pleasant. Make some suggestions: You know it bothers him that you sometimes leave the dishes in the sink overnight, or you know he would like to have a nice quiet grown-up dinner one night a week without the baby food and the spilled milk. Or you might offer to make it possible for him to have complete privacy and homemade snacks for Monday night football if he would be willing to set aside another night of the week for family night.

He may come up with some suggestions of his own, things that you never imagined might be important to him. And here's where you might have to go back to our first step and watch out for defensiveness. He might suggest that he would gladly have family night once a week if you would promise never to wear that horrible green dress in public again, or if you would just stop cooking goulash every Wednesday. Don't lose sight of your goal — it's a workable compromise!

In your zeal to get family night established, don't make any promises you won't be able to keep. Mutual-profit bargaining is not only a means to a compromise; it's a terrific vehicle for self-improvement. If you promise that you'll clean up the sink every night before you go to bed, you've got to *do* it, otherwise your bargaining power will be gone and you won't be able to blame your husband if the family night idea fizzles.

Learn your job description and do your job. Avoid being defensive. Express your feelings, and listen to your husband's feelings. Bargain for mutual profit. These don't sound much like the pretty words you often find in books about love and eternal happiness. But after you've experienced the terrific feelings that come from playing the game fairly and honestly, you can write the pretty and sentimental love stories yourself!

Chapter 6
Robots, Parrots, or Personalities?

Dear Jenny:

Thanks for your note and that darling birth announcement. I'm thrilled for you! I'm making something for the baby – I'll send it when I get finished. Brad's eight months old now; I think he's going to grow up to be an athlete like his dad. He can crawl! I'm enclosing some pictures.

Thanks for asking about my philosophy of child rearing. I think it's so important that we crystallize our thinking while our children are young, don't you? Next to love and security, I think a stimulating environment is the key. I've constructed a fabulous mobile in the crib, where if the baby pulls one string he'll ring the bells, and if he pulls another he'll rattle the rattles. And I let him watch Sesame Street from the infant seat.

No, Jenny, I haven't softened my feelings toward play pens. Pens are for chickens and pigs! A child needs room to explore, or else how will he ever learn to control his environment? These early years can mean a difference of ten to twenty I.Q. points! Oh, Jenny, it's such an awesome chal-

lenge to be given this little mind to teach, this little spirit to nourish!

Love,
Afton

September 22, 1970

Dear Jenny:

Congratulations, both on the new baby and the darling birth announcement! I am sending the gift I made for Shelley; maybe she won't mind sharing it with her new brother. I hope they like the building blocks with the Greek alphabet letters. They're painted with non-toxic paint, so it's okay if they chew.

Our Kristin is adorable. She is such a good baby; plays in her playpen for hours. We had to get a playpen to protect her from her older brother and the dog. They're both fine. I'll send pictures when we take some – maybe Christmas.

Love,
Afton

January 9, 1977

Dear Jenny:

Thanks for the pictures you sent with your Christmas letter. Your five children are beautiful, and growing so quickly.

You asked whether my philosophy of child rearing had changed since we were in school together. What's a philosophy?

I especially liked the picture of Shelley and her ice hockey team. Remember how you swore you would only buy your daughter feminine toys and lacy dresses so she wouldn't get confused about her sex role? Brad's playing the violin. His dad had a fit when the idea first came up, but he's having a lot of fun with it now. Weren't we silly, thinking all there was to raising kids was to mold a piece of plastic clay into a nice clean-cut form? Who would have guessed that those little people we called our babies had so much personality of their own? I guess it has something to do with the preexistence.

Keep in touch.

Love,
Afton

I guess we all look on in disbelief sometimes when we find ourselves replacing our solemnly sworn "I will always . . ." or "I will never . . ." with the nearest available means of coping with a situation. It's a very rigid mother who doesn't make such a switch, because even the most carefully thought-out plans and theories must be altered when they don't fit the needs of a particular child in a particular situation.

Mothering is probably more of an art than a science.

Some artists seem to have been born absolutely and completely talented. For example, when I heard that Mozart composed his first symphony at the age of eight, and that Handel composed the *Messiah* in less than twenty-five days, I was stunned. Some artists are so talented that they become great without ever having had a lesson and, it seems, without having to touch up, rewrite, or start over. Some of these artists contend that formal classes or lessons would have had a weakening influence on their own creativity. I'm sure I'd never venture to discuss whether they were wrong or right — I can't argue with greatness.

Other artists have talent, but they find that in order to develop that talent to a level of greatness, or near greatness, they have to study and practice and learn and relearn. They go to school, they take classes and lessons. They work with those who can help them to refine their abilities. By learning the laws of their discipline they are better able to express their own ideas or feelings.

Others are born with little of the substance we call talent or natural ability, but they have a love for art. They study, they work, they fail, they start again. If they study hard enough and are single-minded in their labor, they can reach a level of achievement which will bring them happiness and allow them to share with others. They may or may not reach a level of performance that is recognized as great or near great, but they will achieve.

It's the same with mothers. Some women reach adulthood with an abundance of love, patience, understanding, and common sense. They seem almost instinctively to do the right things, and when they make mistakes it doesn't matter because they know how to forgive themselves. Who knows whether a knowledge of Gessell's stages of development or a practicum in client-centered therapy would have enhanced their already well-developed sense of mothering? Neither they nor their happy families ever stopped to ask.

These are the Mozarts and Handels of the mothering profession. But for some reason most women think that all mothers should fit into that category. Well, maybe they should — but they don't!

Many women find that they have some talent for mothering. Most of the time they may be warm, understanding, patient, and loving. They may have a natural love for children, or the ability to teach or to inspire or to comfort. They may find that they have plenty of warmth but not much patience; or a lot of creativity but not much energy. There is room for improvement, and they are usually willing to put forth the effort.

Other women swear that they have no, that is NO talent for mothering. They are not, they insist, the type! They may have excelled in another profession, or they may be trying to figure out just where their niche can be. They may be efficient, artistic, brilliant, or just living from one day to the next, but they are convinced that they would register ½ on a scale of 1 to 10 of mothering abilities. They never liked baby-sitting, or even babies for that matter, and they would rather be a custodian than teach a class of three-year-olds.

To you who feel that mothering is definitely not your strong suit, but who find yourself in the role of mother, don't sell yourself short. It's true you may never get a big thrill out of baking cookies or knitting booties, but that's all right. Just as you've discovered that having a child of your own is not like baby-sitting for the woman up the street, you'll discover that there are other ways of great mothering than making quilts and running for PTA president. Now that you know the feeling that comes from the realization that your child (who is, strangely, much more appealing than all those other children you ever knew) has only you to provide for his physical and emotional needs, you will find your own ways of providing love and warmth, because you'll want to.

Those of us who do not fit into the born-genius category of gifted mothers will find, like the talented-but-not-yet-polished and not-so-talented-but-determined artists, that we can increase the quality of our mothering with a little help. Help is available from (1) your Father in heaven, (2) your own untapped resources, and (3) professionals.

Your Father in heaven. I once heard of an LDS child psychologist who was asked, "Of all the methods of teaching and behavior control you have discussed, which do you use in your home?" He answered: "None of them. When we have a problem in our home we call upon the Lord, and he tells us what to do."

While traveling through Champaign, Illinois, I noticed a huge billboard advertising a hot-line for harried parents. There was a number that a mother could call whenever she came upon a problem she didn't know how to deal with, or whenever she needed some support to be consistent in her discipline, or when she just needed someone to tell her that she wasn't crazy and that things would probably be better tomorrow. Someone would answer the telephone who had had some education in how to parent, and they would give support and ideas. I thought this was a good idea.

Wouldn't it be terrific if we had a direct line to speak with Haim Ginott or Rudolf Dreikurs, or another popular authority on parent-child relationships? Especially if they said: "Look — call any time! I don't care if it's three o'clock in the morning; I want to hear from you." Wouldn't we then be able to handle our little problems in a much more mature and healthy way?

I guess that what the LDS child psychologist was saying is that he *has* a direct line; not to a writer who, for all his inspiration, is limited in his scope of knowledge and understanding, but to the Creator, who is completely familiar not only with all the laws of human behavior but with the little individual personality quirks of each mother and father and child on the earth. A contact like that could really prove helpful!

It's a relationship well worth cultivating.

Your own untapped resources. Common sense, woman's intuition, mother love — whatever it is called, each of us has a reservoir of good judgment and inspiration that is ours to help us in making those on-the-spot decisions or preventing impending disaster. If we don't seem to be able to recognize these gifts, it may be because we are so concerned with what others believe, or what we have read, that we have lost confidence in our own ability to do what is right.

Learn to listen to your inner self.

The professionals. Some people contend that because we have the gift of the Holy Ghost, and because we have common sense, we don't need to bother ourselves with books on child development and behavior. Some people adopt the attitude of "Them versus Us," "Them" being those who do behavioral research and write books (representing the worldly influence), and "Us" being those who know the truth.

I personally feel that an awareness of the discoveries that are being made in the field of human relationships has been helpful to me as a mother. Although I do recognize the tremendous help that I can receive from my Heavenly Father, I feel that he is pleased when I do what I can on my own. When my child asks for help with a school assignment I am delighted to help him. I'm glad that he thinks I am smart enough to interpret a fourth-grade social studies book, and I am glad that we have the kind of relationship that will allow him to come to me when he needs help. But when he asks me for help on every step of the assignment I am inclined to say "Read the directions!" I think that the Lord expects me to read the directions and learn all I can, and that he will gladly fill in the gaps and add enlightenment when it is necessary.

It *is* important to have the guidance of our Father in heaven as we study. It will help us to recognize half-truths and false teachings for what they are, the best that a particular writer could do to interpret the facts within his framework of understanding. That guidance will also help us to recognize eternal truths whether we run across them in a science book or a book of poetry. I have felt a witness of truth that gave me goosebumps and brought tears to my eyes while reading a non-Mormon author's interpretation of respect for free agency and individuality.

When I answered my friend Jenny's inquiry about my philosophy of child-rearing I might have been less facetious. I might have said that, while I am no longer adamant about play pens and coloring books, and while I no longer profess to be really consistent in anything except my inconsistencies, my basic philosophy hasn't changed. My "philosophy" is made of the things I value: love, freedom, communication, tolerance, self-discipline, humor, happiness. My hope is to teach my children to respect themselves, love the Lord, and appreciate others. I want my children to learn to do what is right because they know it's best for them, not just because they want to make me happy. I don't want to create a robot that I can program to be proper and polite, because if he is dependent upon me now he may later be dependent upon someone less concerned with his welfare. I don't want to train a parrot who might say what he knows I want to hear; I want to help to educate a mind, a spirit. And while I'm at this awesome task, I hope to be able to sit back, sometimes, and just enjoy getting acquainted with a young person who has a personality all his own.

Chapter 7

The Sixth
September

◇o◁—————————————————————————

This is the first year since my children started school that I have lived through a completely calm September, without a fit of depression or the fear that I would never be able to live through the following nine months. I don't mean to imply that I've been pregnant every fall; it's just that I get a serious case of the back-to-school jitters. I can't remember feeling that way when *I* was in school, but then I was mainly concerned with whether we'd play jump-rope or hopscotch at recess. *I* didn't have to worry about my delicate self-image, my social adjustment, or my Metropolitan Achievement Test score!

When my son started kindergarten I was beside myself because there were thirty-five kids in his class. I was sure that either the teacher would become so distraught under the pressure that she[1] would one day plant a time bomb under the workbench, or she would lose track of my son on one of the

---

[1]Throughout I refer to the teacher as she because "he or she" is a clumsy construction anyway and because there are more female elementary-school teachers than male. I expect to continue this usage until I discover a neuter pronoun with more human overtones than "it."

field trips and leave him stranded in the lavatory at the fire station.

The first week of first grade he complained of excruciating stomach pains; they were so serious that he lay in the back seat groaning all the way to the doctor. When the doctor found him in excellent health and Brad looked sheepish, I was appalled that School Anxiety had, after all my precautions, actually stricken Our Home. The next year my daughter, Kristin, started kindergarten, and my defenses were alerted on the first day when, in a sex-identity crisis, the teacher's assistant told me she had tried to discourage my *son*, *Chris*, from spending all his time in the housekeeping corner!

Every September I worry that the teacher doesn't know how to teach, or that she will never learn to see the bright mind and beautiful soul that I send to her in faded levis and school sweatshirt. Every June I send a thank-you note filled with love and appreciation to an outstanding teacher who has given her own special gifts to my child, her adoring pupil.

This September was better. I think I'm finally adjusting to school!

As a former teacher and parent education group leader, I should like to share some rules of thumb which might be helpful as you live through the elementary school years with your children. As a mother, who knows that the heart is higher than the thumbs, I will, with you, continue to be shocked and surprised as my children manage to present an exception to every rule I subscribe to.

ADVICE FROM A TEACHER

If you wait until your child starts kindergarten or first grade before being concerned about his intellectual development, you've missed a great opportunity. Where education is concerned, the greatest gift a child can receive from his parents is an inquiring mind and an unquenchable desire for knowledge. These traits aren't really learned, they're assimilated. Many mothers spend a lot of time and effort coaching their children to memorize the alphabet and numbers, whereas observing nature, performing simple experiments, or enjoying story books and verse normally would lay a much more firm base for education.

Children have an incredible desire to be like their parents, even when their parents aren't the kind of people they want their children to be. I was assigned to test a child who was brought to a clinic for exceptional children by his parents because he couldn't read. We found his I.Q. to be normal, and he didn't display any evidence of what the schools now call learning disability. Upon interviewing his parents we found that his father never read the newspaper and his mother never read anything except an occasional recipe. He had never seen his parents read! We advised his parents and his teacher to give him an opportunity to see those people he cared about reading something.

An elementary school I know sets aside twenty minutes a day for silent reading. During this time not only the children but the teachers, the secretaries, and the principal (and perhaps even the cooks and janitors) are required to read. This is done because many of the children come from homes where adults watch television but do not read, and the principal feels that the children need an opportunity to see respected adults reading for pleasure. So the next time you feel guilty about reading a book instead of scrubbing the floor, take heart. At least in one area you can claim to be setting a good example!

Another way you can help to prepare your child for school is to teach him to be self-directed and independent. Teachers make jokes about overprotective mothers who boast that their children are well-mannered, well-behaved, and sweet. The children of such mothers sometimes prove well-mannered and well-behaved under the mother's direct supervision, but may be either belligerent and unmanageable or shy and fearful around a parent substitute. Such children may be well disciplined by their own private disciplinarian, but they are not self-disciplined. A self-disciplined child is able to behave appropriately even out of the reaches of adult supervision.

SUGGESTIONS FROM A PARENT EDUCATOR

When your child does start school, remember — it's his education, not yours!

A child learns to take responsibility when the assignment or project is clearly *his responsibility*. When parents nag, beg, threaten, or give excessive amounts of help, they make the assignments their responsibility!

> *Example*: Sally comes home from school carrying her math book.
> Mother: Hi, Sally! Do you have math to do today?
> Sally: Yes, I've got to do a page of multiplication.
> Mother: Well, get on it immediately. I want you to do your math before you do anything else.

Why is it important to Mother that Sally complete her assignment? Perhaps because she wants to teach Sally to be dependable, or perhaps because she knows Sally is sensitive and will be crushed if she is reprimanded by the teacher. Alternatively, it may be that Mother doesn't want the teacher to think, ''What a careless mother that is, to let her child come to school without completing her assignment!''

> *Example*: Supper time, and Sally has not completed her math. She has created a magnificent doodle, bitten off all her fingernails, and unravelled her left stocking, but she has done only a few math problems.
> Mother: Sally, is your math done?
> Sally: Not quite, Mother. Just about.
> Mother: You're not to play or watch television until you're all through.
> Sally: Yes, Mother.

The same dialogue takes place a little before bedtime. Finally Sally is sent to bed with the promise (or threat) that Mother will get her up early to work on her math.

The next morning mother panics and so does Sally. Mother, sleepy and irritable, sits down with Sally to make sure she works on her math. When Father and the children wake up, Sally is furious because Mother has to prepare breakfast and cannot continue to help her. Mother is furious because Sally had all the previous evening to do her math in and still isn't finished. Father is furious because Mother and Sally are fighting. The children are furious because Mother only has time to prepare a cereal they don't particularly like. Sally, tearfully and belligerently, berates Mother for not getting her up early enough.

What Mother doesn't know, and what probably even Sally doesn't know, is that Mother has allowed Sally to engage her in an unnecessary power-struggle. Mother represents power; Sally represents someone who doesn't like to be overpowered. In completing the assignment when she is told, Sally bows to her mother's power. In not completing the assignment when she is told, she shows her own power. It's not until the last minute that Sally becomes more concerned with the real problem, i.e., finishing her math, than with the game she and Mother are playing.

Even then, Sally has not lost completely. She has won an hour or so of her mother's undivided attention, and she has caused her mother to feel guilty and upset. If Mother's goal was to teach Sally to be dependable, she has failed; it is Mother who has learned to have assignments in on time. If it was her goal to protect Sally from a reprimand from her teacher she has succeeded, but she has damaged her own relationship with Sally in the process. If it was her goal to appear to be the "good" parent she has succeeded, unless the teacher notices that Sally is tired and irritable in class after frequent homework episodes at home.

Sally's mother needs to allow Sally to take responsibility

for her own homework. She might help Sally to fix up a quiet place to work, or she might help Sally to plan her after-school schedule to include a time for homework. Then she should show Sally that she trusts her to complete her homework by leaving her alone. If Sally doesn't complete an assignment, she should be allowed to suffer the consequences. The assignment is between Sally and the teacher.

CONFESSIONS OF A MOTHER

I want to believe you, Parent Educator, and in the main I do. What you say makes a lot of sense. But I have one or two reservations. It's true that the individual assignment is between Sally and the teacher, but the total education is not — that is between her and her parents. And since too many unfinished assignments make a poor education, the parent might at some point feel compelled to step in.

That's the long-term view, of course. It seems to me that the parent has to try to assess the immediate problem, the real problem, and act accordingly. If the problem is a power struggle, with the parent asserting authority and the child playing tactical games to resist her, the most likely result is a deteriorating parent-child relationship. In that case reestablishing the relationship becomes more important right now than the child's getting assignments completed, or even than any immediate need for him to develop responsibility. Then the "hands-off" route is the way to go, at least until the relationship improves, just as that route would seem to be a likely incentive to responsibility where no power struggle at all was involved.

Yes, the natural consequences principle is a good one. It should work that way in practice, but oh, how many times I've had to witness that last-minute panic because I had kept myself from nagging and begging and insisting and helping on the previous evening. Although I've managed to maintain my "it's your problem" stance, the torn feeling inside has told me that my method of teaching responsibility was not working as I had intended. One of my children was created to operate on the principle of natural consequences; the two of us work together just like the "how to" examples I have read. But the other was born with a genius for challenging my attempt to remove myself from a situation. I find myself in a power struggle in just trying to avoid a power struggle!

One of the reasons why I determined never to get involved in my children's schoolwork is that as a teacher I had seen what can happen when a well-meaning but uptight parent assumes too much responsibility for teaching at home. I have actually seen a child have an asthma attack or burst into tears at the sight of a reading book because the pressure to read has become unbearable. Less serious, I have seen children confused because they were taught different material by a different method at home, and they couldn't reconcile their home instruction with their school instruction.

But my children's teachers don't always share my philosophy. Often teachers give science assignments, for example, that are supposed to be family projects. It is not unusual for a teacher to request that a parent help a child with reading, number facts, or handwriting. As my children grow and I see that the "hands off completely" approach isn't entirely practical, given my personality and my kids and their school, I'm constantly looking for new ways to help *without* taking the responsibility from my child.

In trying to determine why the natural consequences approach hasn't always had positive results in our home, I am reminded of the time when the Lord rescinded the gift of translation from Oliver Cowdery because of Oliver's failure to study and pray concerning the translation. "Behold, you have not understood; you have supposed that I would give it unto you, when you took no thought save it was to ask me." (D&C 9:7.) Then the Lord goes on to tell of the effort that is necessary in order to make translations, even *with* heavenly help. I had assumed that the only necessary element in teaching children by natural consequences was to keep out of their business, to refuse to get involved. I now believe that I should have more carefully seen to it that my children had pre-school experiences where they learned responsibility, and I should have adopted a more supportive manner of withholding help. Fortunately, none of my power has been rescinded, except as I have lost it through my own ineffectiveness.

Another thing I have discovered is that my children love my attention, and they will take it in any way, shape, or form. I wonder whether the power struggle that takes place when I adopt the "don't get involved" approach isn't a means of getting me involved in one way or another. I find that when I agree to get involved to some extent at first, my child is much more responsible for his assignment in the long run.

Occasionally now I will sit and listen to my son practice the violin, and nearly always I listen to my daughter read. I am constructing materials to help them in the areas in which their teachers have asked me to help, and my children are delighted. Perhaps one thing I have done right is to let the children know that I am helping them because they want help, or feel a need for help, and not because I wish to control their lives.

But what if the parent feels she knows better how to teach her child than the teacher does?

This brings up a different way in which parents seem to be unable to let go. They become upset because the school is too permissive or progressive, or because it doesn't seem to be up on modern educational developments. They are worried because the teacher puts too much stress on handwriting, or not enough. They don't like the "open classroom" approach, or they are afraid that teaching machines will soon replace teachers. It doesn't matter how much or how little we know about education; we all have our suspicions and our fears.

Obviously, from my battle with the back-to-school jitters, suspicions and fears are not completely outside the realm of my experience. But I know that in a parent-school situation, as in any other area of life, suspicions and fears can be extremely harmful. I would suggest that if you are anything less than pleased with your school, you outline a program of education for yourself that will help you to be more comfortable with your child's school. Here is my own lesson plan:

Objective: I will establish a positive relationship with my child's teacher and other school personnel.

Learning experiences:

1. Attend all school meetings and parent-teacher conferences.
2. Do not, under any condition, allow yourself to become defensive or aggressive with school personnel.
3. Volunteer to help.

1. *Attend all school meetings and parent-teacher conferences.* It is important that you know my innermost thoughts and feelings lest you are tempted to cringe at the foregoing suggestions.

When I taught school I categorized the PTA as an organization for bored and lonely adults who had nothing better to do than to plan panel discussions and bake sales. I attended the monthly meetings because I had to, and every time we recited the PTA pledge I made a pledge of my own never to darken the door of a PTA meeting when I retired from the teaching profession. Meanwhile, I enjoyed the learning materials and playground equipment that somehow resulted from the bake sales and carnivals.

I might never have been trapped into going to another PTA meeting if they hadn't offered ice cream to the class who had the largest number of parents in attendance. Thinking unkind thoughts about the shameless attendance committee who had exploited the innocence of childhood as a foolproof advertising gimmick, I listened to the endless financial reports and motions to amend. I cringed at the realization that a baby-sitter for a PTA meeting charges the same hourly rate as a baby sitter for dinner at Garabaldi's.

Now, five years later, I attend regularly. You expect me to say, no doubt, that I now sit with bated breath to hear the report of the ways and means committee or the extent to which the nutritional content of the school lunch complies with the minimum daily requirement. Not so. I have simply determined that the opportunity I have to meet with school personnel and other parents and to feel the pulse of the school, together with the mystic way that my presence at these meetings seems to lend some kind of "support" to the school, makes it worth a dollar an hour for a sitter and an evening of less than spine-tingling excitement. Feeling comfortable about my school and knowing that the faculty is a group of likeable, honest, intelligent people means a lot to me as a parent.

2. *Do not, under any condition, allow yourself to become defensive or aggressive with school personnel.* Assertive, maybe, but not aggressive.

As I sit in back-to-school night and watch anxious parents launch a verbal attack on a teacher about whether she spends thirty minutes or forty minutes a day on math, or about the virtues of Scott-Forsman over the Ginn Reading Series, I thank heaven for the sense of perspective I am gaining with age. Through my experience as a teacher and as an involved parent I have discovered that most teachers have the welfare of their students at heart, and most of them are well qualified to do their jobs. This is becoming more true as teaching positions become less available and school systems are blessed with a larger number of qualified applicants to choose from.

There are exceptions, of course, and I admit that, on occasions when I have felt that my child would have trouble adjusting to a teacher with certain personality traits, I have requested that the child be assigned to another teacher's class. But now that my children have had successful beginning school years they are becoming increasingly able to deal with opposition, and now that I am becoming better acquainted with the faculty at our school I am becoming more convinced that there isn't a teacher in the group that couldn't give my children something valuable.

If you do have a problem you are concerned about, by all means bring it to the teacher's attention. This should be done in the privacy of a prearranged parent-teacher conference and in a matter-of-fact, non-attacking manner. The trouble with putting the teacher on the defensive is that she may develop ill feelings toward you. (Perhaps also toward your child, if you're too obnoxious. It's unfortunate, but there is an element of humanness in the best of teachers.) This will result in a power struggle rather than in a united attempt to remedy the situation. The teacher will probably be delighted to work with you if she perceives you as a person asking for help, but she may be inclined to fight back if she sees you as an attacker.

3. *Volunteer to help.* I used to think of volunteers in the same terms as I thought of PTA attenders, only more so. I thought that women served on committees and helped in the clinic because they had a Florence Nightingale complex or because they were frustrated socialites. Look at me now: always a room mother, twice a team mother, and a regular Thursday morning tutor in the language lab.

Volunteering at school has the same benefits as attending PTA meetings, since it helps a mother to become acquainted with the school, its staff, its policies, and its problems. In addition, it helps the school to extend its services beyond those covered by local government funds.

Our school district announced that in the 1975-76 school year 24,495 volunteers contributed an estimated two million dollars' worth of work hours. Many schools are most grateful for mothers to help in the classroom, in tutoring projects, doing typing or dittoing, constructing materials, or supervising in the lunchroom or on the playground. It may not be the career you've always dreamed of, and if you have several preschool children it may not fit into your present job description. But if you have a question about the effectiveness of your school ask yourself: Will I be a part of the problem or part of the solution?

Chapter 8

Got Your Ears On?

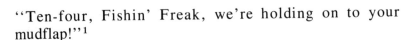

"Ten-four, Fishin' Freak, we're holding on to your mudflap!"[1]

Our trip to Utah last summer was our family's most exciting vacation ever. We camped, we fished, we swam, and we worked, as we caught up on the past two years with family and friends. But the highlight of the trip was when we traded our trusty station wagon for a new pickup truck, complete with protective shell and CB radio.

On the way back to Virginia, the Wyoming desert didn't seem so barren and the Kansas cornfields didn't seem so endless as we listened to the friendly exchanges between truck drivers in the accent they had adopted to add authenticity to their already complicated jargon. We answered self-consciously as our presence on the road was acknowledged with a "Breaker one-nine, breaker one-nine! Got your ears on, Good Buddy?"

The listening wasn't always easy. Not only were we

---

[1]Translation: "Message received, Fishin' Freak, we're right behind you."

unaccustomed to the language of this exclusive group, but we found the accents of the long-time professionals difficult to understand. This, added to the static caused by heavy expressway traffic, caused us all to sit on the edges of our seats, listening with concentrated effort.

Two elements were necessary for us to keep up with the transmitted dialogue: Our undivided attention, and the ability to decode. These, I believe, are exactly the elements which we as parents need to keep in touch with our children.

When a baby is just learning to talk, his mother waits anxiously for him to form his first words. When he utters a sound she watches his face carefully, using sight as well as hearing in an attempt to make words out of the sounds he utters. As he increases his vocabulary but speaks in a complicated baby-talk, complete with his own original sound substitutions, she learns to discriminate between childish chatter and a real need to communicate, and she looks and listens intently in an attempt to interpret his speech when interpretation is necessary.

As children grow and their speech becomes clearer, mothers usually develop the ability to listen as they work. "How was school today, dear? You can tell me while I peel these potatoes!" She is not realizing that the back of Mother's head is not a responsive audience. "Keep talking, honey, I can hear you . . ." she says, as she moves from room to room.

Of course, a mother can't listen intently to every child all the time. With only two children, I find that they are both competing for my undivided attention whenever we are in close quarters, like the same room or the car. I am sure the problem is multiplied by each additional child. And there are household chores, and telephones, and meetings, and the need to be alone sometimes. So since we can't possibly listen intently *all the time*, it is important that we make sure we listen intently and completely to *each* of our children at *some time* during each day.

As with a CB radio, we not only need to have our ears on but we need to have our antennae up. We should sharpen our sixth sense, be it mother's intuition, inspiration, or simply a sensitivity to the needs of others, and use it always as we deal with our children. I have a friend who says that when she is spiritually in tune she can always tell when there is something bothering one of her children.

I had an astonishing experience with a silent call for help many years ago when I was working in Salt Lake City and living with a girl friend. She had gone out for the evening and I had gone to bed. When *I* go to bed, I am settled in for the night. I sleep very soundly. But on this particular night when my friend came into the room I woke up suddenly, with a very frightened, almost electrifying sensation. She hadn't said a word, but I knew as soon as she entered the room that she had had a frightening experience and needed to talk about it. We are entitled to such promptings; we should use them.

When we listen to our children intently it should be with our whole bodies. First, we must look directly into their eyes. This is easiest when we are at about the same height as they are, so if you are talking with a young child you may need to kneel on the floor or pick him up. For good communication you don't want to have to "look down on" the speaker and he should not have to look up to you.

Physical contact usually helps to increase the level of communication. Holding a young child on your lap or putting your arm around the shoulder of an older one may have a comforting effect that says "I want to be close to you." Just holding hands is sometimes effective. Teach your whole body to say "warmth and closeness"; this will probably do more than any mode of questioning or verbal response to encourage a sharing of feelings.

Of course, the ability to listen *completely* is of great importance. If you want to encourage your child to talk, turn off the broiler or take the cookies out of the oven so that you won't be interrupted by the urgency of your household tasks in the middle of a heart-to-heart talk. Do whatever you can to assure your ability to keep your mind on the conversation. These little talks will possibly mean more to your present and future relationship with your child than all the cookies you will ever bake or all the family outings you will ever plan.

Although your undivided attention is probably the most important element in communication, the way parents respond to children's comments can have a great deal to do with the level of helpfulness of a conversation. Just as dentists are trying to impress people to brush correctly and use dental floss, and as doctors sponsor commercials to urge people to eat right and avoid accidents, the counseling profession has shared some of its secrets as its contribution to "preventative therapy." With dedication and practice, a mother now can learn to become an effective sounding-board for her children, to help them express their feelings and solve their own problems.

There are many ways a mother can respond to her children's sharing of problems. *For example*: Your child comes home from school obviously out of sorts. She stomps into the house and throws her coat on the couch, crying, "Nobody likes me!" Here are some of the ways that you might respond:

Questions: Who doesn't like you? What happened to make you feel that way?

Laughing it off: Cheer up! Tomorrow you will have forgotten all about it. I'll get you a snack and you can watch The After School Special.

Explaining: We all think that sometimes. Probably it just seemed that no one likes you because of something that happened at school today. Children can be cruel to each other without thinking about it.

Insisting: Stop having such a negative attitude! No one *will* like you if you go around with such a long face all the time!

Pollyanna-ing: Nonsense, sweetheart! *I* like you! Your Daddy likes you! Grandma and Grandpa like you, and Heavenly Father likes you!

Advising: Well, let's see what we can do to make you more popular. . . .

Criticizing: Why must you *always* come in like that and ruin the day for the rest of us?

Sugar-coating: A lovely girl like you? Who could resist that beautiful smile and your cute sense of humor? I'm sure *someone* likes you. . . .

Some of the above responses are negative, while some *appear* to be quite positive. But none of them pave the way for further exploration of the problem. The counselor-mother must find a way to provide an opportunity for the child to (1) talk about her problem, (2) convince *herself* that things are not hopeless, and (3) discover a possible solution to her problem.

Mothers can learn to do this through reflective listening. In reflective listening you have to listen intently and think about what has been said, then interpret it in your own words. If your daughter has just said "Nobody likes me!" and you believe this is her way of telling you she has a problem and would like some help, follow her lead. Interpret what she has said.

"You feel as if all your friends have deserted you."

You must be careful not to belittle in any way the importance or truth of what has been said. You know that at least someone likes her, but the counselor's job is not to convince; it is to listen and interpret. Beware that there might be the least little bit of teasing or ridicule in your voice. Strive for a matter-of-fact honest attempt to reflect what the child says.

We interpret for two reasons. First, to make sure we know what the child is really feeling. Second, to give the child an opportunity to tell us more about the problem. Sometimes your interpretation will be wrong, but if it is stated in a way that says "I'm really trying to figure out what you are worried about, so that I can help you" your child will try to clarify her feelings. For example:

Daughter: Nobody likes me!

Mother: You feel as if all your friends have deserted you.

Daughter: It's not just friends. My teachers don't even like me!

(Aha! You're beginning to see some direction! But resist the impulse to ask, "What happened to make you think one of your teachers doesn't like you?" Asking isn't interpreting, and it might turn the discussion into an interrogation session.)

Mother: It's mostly the teachers that have made you feel let down.

Even after all my years as the wife of a professional counselor plus teaching this skill in parent education groups, it is difficult for me to come up with responses that don't either sound funny or end with a question mark. People in our parent groups seem to have the same problem. Learning a different way to respond to children is like learning a new language or learning to walk backwards; it takes a lot of practice and experience. Some of our group members worry that their teenagers look at them questioningly and say: "Mom! What are you doing?" But even when the children laugh at the clumsy ways the parents find themselves interpreting at first, they seem to appreciate the fact that the parents have taken the initiative toward a better relationship, especially when the parents explain that they are trying to become better listeners. Teenagers have funny ways of expressing their reactions. Your child may be thinking "I've got to hand it to you, Mom, you'll try anything," when what she says is *"Weird!"* Don't be intimidated.

Using reflective listening with your young children has

the advantage that by the time the children become teenagers and the need to communicate is urgent, you will have developed your counseling abilities to a high degree. Young children don't seem to mind how awkward you sound, as long as you are willing to sit still and listen to them. Young children can profit tremendously from the opportunity to express their feelings to a mother-counselor who is willing to listen with her mind as well as with her heart.

The only way to perfect your skill at reflective listening is to do it every day. Not in every situation, of course. When your son comes in to ask what happened to his skateboard, you don't need to say "You're worried because you can't find your skateboard." Knowing when to reflect and when to answer is part of the listening skill. Try to determine when your child is really saying "I need to talk to someone," then get the counselor gear going. When children are given a chance to express their feelings in a non-judgmental atmosphere, you'll find that there is less whining, less fighting, and fewer of those countless games children play to get attention.

One day when I had had an upsetting experience with a friend, I was amply rewarded for my attempts at reflective listening. I was hurt and angry as the family got into the car for an outing. Briefly I told my husband what had happened, and my seven-year-old said, in a most facilitating tone of voice, "You're hurt because Sister Burton didn't include you in her plans!"

Ten-four?

Chapter 9

Nobody Wins in a Power Struggle

◇○◁──────────────────────────

"In this corner, wearing a blue robe, and weighing in at one hundred and twenty-nine pounds, is Mother.

"And in this corner, wearing red feet-in sleepers, and weighing in at thirty-one pounds, is Bradley.

"Ladies and gentlemen, this is highly irregular. The contestants seem to be most unevenly matched. I am awaiting word from the commissioner to see whether there has been some mistake. But wait, ladies and gentlemen! In spite of her tremendous weight advantage, Mother is becoming agitated. Her face is turning red. Her breath is coming in short, labored gasps. It can't be — it is! Little Bradley is wearing her down. Ladies and gentlemen, I see it but I don't believe it. Mother, in spite of her advantage in terms of weight and experience, is overwhelmed. Her resistance is rapidly being worn down by Bradley, the determined and resilient two-year-old. The referee is counting; Mother seems to have given up. Ladies and gentlemen, the winner . . . !"

I've come a long way in the art of avoiding and ending power struggles since my first encounters with the tyrannical tricks of a two-year-old. I thought I'd conquered my thirst for power and that "come out fighting" instinct until the other day when I was a substitute teacher at our neighborhood school. Then it all came back. The first child to dispute my authority awakened those same old fighting urges. I heard myself snap, "*I'll* tell you when you can go to the bathroom!" before I realized what was happening. I took a deep breath and laughed at the picture of myself, poised for battle against an innocent, if somewhat rebellious, first-grader.

The power struggle is perhaps the greatest offender in husband-wife and mother-child relationships, yet it is often the most difficult to escape. Although I have been successful in my attempt to cut down the number of ultimatums I deliver, and although I have, at least to some degree, convinced my son and daughter that a workable solution is more advantageous than a marathon to have it his way or her way, sometimes I still catch myself playing the "me-against-you game" without the ability to see what is happening. I will have arrived — I mean really *arrived* — as a wife and mother as soon as I learn to keep out of power struggles.

When that happens, maybe I'll understand what the Savior meant when he said, "And whosoever shall compel thee to go a mile, go with him twain." (Matthew 5:41.) Right now I have trouble following that advice. If Whosoever asked nicely, I'd be glad to go the second mile. But when he starts compelling, watch out!

Maybe I could do it if I had my adrenal glands removed; because it's not that I don't know all the rules for avoiding and withdrawing from power struggles. I do. The problem is that competitive urge that surges through me when my authority is challenged or I see that I might be taken advantage of. It's the bugle call that awakens that old fighting instinct — that's what makes it hard for me sometimes to go the first, let alone the second, mile.

Not that I'm against competition. I've lent much motherly support from the sidelines of a football or soccer game or from the bleachers in the heat of the baseball season.

My husband and I even sponsor a superstar party each year to determine which of our adult friends is to be the champion all-round game player. But there is no prize for the daily fight for power that is the cause of most of the discomfort and contention within a family.

Power struggles don't happen just between outgoing, assertive-type people, either. Some of the most harmful power struggles are fought under the guise of quietness and softness as they play on feelings of guilt or indebtedness. It's simply that some power struggles are better disguised than others.

The urge to win seems to be inherent within us, and that's a wonderful thing. I want to be a winner; I want my children to learn to be winners. In games and sports someone has to lose in order for someone else to win. In life, the real winners learn the art of winning without doing so at someone else's expense. In the fine art of parenting (or partnering, or brothering or sistering) the best way to deal with the inevitable power struggle is to turn it into a winning situation for both parties involved. Yes, it's possible!

The first step in avoiding a power struggle is to learn to recognize one when it appears. All power struggles are the same in that two (it could be more, but to keep it simple we'll say two) people are pitted against each other. Each has the same goal: to win, or to be boss. The contest for power can be manifest in hundreds of ways. Some are:

In Children	*In Parents*
Arguing	Arguing
Fighting	Force
Temper tantrums	Punishment
Refusal to work	Authoritarianism
Crying	Insisting
Showing off	Shouting
Disobedience	Shaming
Rebellion	Threatening

I was once told that the easiest way to recognize a power struggle is to analyze your own feelings. When you feel the old fighting spirit, or the urge to "show who is boss," chances are you're into it.

Once you realize that you are in a power struggle, the next step is to get out of it. Sometimes it is practical to simply withdraw; to hand in your ammunition and armor and quit fighting. This is easy to do in a verbal argument when winning or losing doesn't involve any action on your part.

Have you ever discovered yourself arguing with your husband or child about a principle which really doesn't matter anyway? Because of our family's competitive natures, we sometimes argue about such things as whether a certain vocalist has had his teeth capped, or whether or not George Washington really did chop down the cherry tree. Sometimes I take issue with a fact my children believe to be true which I know is not true, and it turns into a mild but irritating disagreement. At such times it is simple enough to withdraw by saying: "I may be wrong. I guess if we really want to know we can go to the source (or the encyclopedia, or the newspaper) and find the truth." In the case of trivia I don't push the importance of finding the right answer.

If you are easy-going, tough-skinned, and slightly hard of hearing you can withdraw from any power struggle and let natural or logical consequences take over. For example: Natural-consequences advocates suggest that when a child refuses to go to bed it is because he wishes to assert his authority and exercise power over his parents. Parents can refuse to play the power game by helping the child get ready for bed, tucking him in, and ignoring any further attempts to keep them busy — such as requests for a drink of water, crying, or peeking around the corner. After a few nights of playing the game alone, the child will decide that he isn't getting much out of the game and that it is best to go to bed at the prescribed time.

Alternatively, if the child chooses to assert himself by

failing to come home when he is called to dinner, Mother simply clears up the dinner dishes after the family is through eating and fails to make special concessions to those who arrive late. Sooner or later the child will decide that going to bed on an empty stomach is a real pain and that it is smart to be on time for meals.

Because it is so completely honest, I believe that the use of natural consequences is a most effective way to teach children to govern their own behavior. It uses learning by experience, and it teaches children to live in accordance with natural laws. I allow my children to learn by natural or logical consequences as often as this is practical. But when a power struggle is involved, I have found that I do not have the calm, unruffled nature (or the sufficiently sturdily-built house) that will allow me to withdraw from all conflicts and ignore all attention-getting behavior.

And when an atmosphere of "me" versus "you" has been established, even the use of logical consequences can cause a power struggle. The child who has been put to bed and ignored may go to great lengths to demand attention from a mother who is equally determined to withhold it; and the child who does not accept missing supper as a logical consequence may beg, plead, or cry for food and thus require his mother to show her power by "holding out." If the mother in question is able to ignore or hold out without developing feelings of desperation or hostility, she is equipped to handle the situation without the elements of a power struggle; in which case, eventually the child will learn the lesson and change his behavior. But if she finds herself thinking "I'll show *you* who's stronger — you'll never get the best of me!" while feelings of anxiety threaten to betray the sweet, calm voice and serene facial expression, she may need to look at some other ways of dealing with the child's unacceptable behavior.

I was delighted when I discovered a way to turn a power contest into a mutually satisfying compromise. I found that instead of ignoring a problem, or copping out, I could end the frustration that both my children and I experienced when we were at odds with one another; and that this was done by working with them to find a solution to the problem which involved some profit for both sides rather than a win for one and a loss for the other.

In this process the conflict is recognized for what it is — a conflict, or an unresolved problem; and the parties involved pool their resources in an attempt to find a solution to the problem which will offer some advantage to each party. After several suggestions have been made each idea is evaluated in terms of equity, and the group (or pair) arrives at one solution which is most likely to work. They then discuss how the solution is to be implemented and provide an alternate plan as a backup.

I discovered this method of problem solving in a book I had brought to keep me busy while my children took swimming lessons at our YWCA. I was immediately given an opportunity to try it out.

Kristin's lesson was in the morning, while Brad's was in the afternoon, so I always packed a sandwich and some fruit for us to eat during the lunch hour. Each child was allowed to buy one item from the vending machines in the hall; they could buy a drink or some crackers to eat with lunch, or they could wait and buy a snack to eat on the way home. But they could not do both.

Brad was five years old at the time, and we were going through that stage where he wanted to buy something every time we went shopping. I felt that he needed to learn to go through a store without satisfying every hungry impulse. He had bought a drink at lunch, and as we prepared to leave the building to go home he asked for some money to buy some candy. Being tired and irritable, I was tempted to give him a dime to keep him quiet, but I knew that that would completely undo all the lessons I had tried to teach about delaying gratification. I said a firm no and braced myself for the half-hour ride home.

My response to whining and temper tantrums had always been one of ignoring. But as I contemplated the noisy ride ahead, I knew I couldn't ignore the begging and pestering for that long a time. I knew what would happen; it had happened before. I would maintain an oblivious and unruffled exterior until the volcano inside would be restrained no longer, then I would cry or scream or spank or shake or do whatever I had to do to vent my own emotions. After that I would spend the rest of the day feeling guilty and ineffective.

Then it hit me. I'd try my new approach to problem solving. I guided the car out of the parking lot and through the one-way streets of the city. When we were out of the traffic I made the big appeal.

"Honey, we've got a very serious problem."

Brad stopped begging and looked interested.

"You want a treat. You want one so badly that you won't take no for an answer. But I don't feel that I can buy you a treat. If I bought a treat I would feel like a bad mother; and besides, I would feel bad about spending that much money. So I won't give in either. There must be *some* way that we could work out our problem so that both of us can feel right about it!"

Brad agreed that we had reached a deadlock and that a compromise would be better than an out-and-out loss. He didn't feel angry, because I hadn't belittled him by moaning about his whining, and he didn't feel defensive because I hadn't asserted my authority. We brainstormed and sifted; and finally we came up with a workable solution. We would go home and make taffy. By doing that I would feel like a good mother, because I would be doing a home-centered activity with my children and not just spending money. Brad would be happy because he would have a treat, and it would be fun getting it. The ride home was pleasant, and the taffy pulling experience proved to be an activity well worth the investment of a couple of hours and a few cups of sugar.

I mentioned this episode to a friend, and she responded: "I could never settle for a compromise like that. I would feel that I had lost!" That's the beauty of the problem-solution method. Someone else could use it and come up with a completely different compromise. I was comfortable with our solution because it contained the elements of delayed gratification (at least for a few hours) and home-centeredness as opposed to commercialization. Someone else might have come up with an equally satisfying compromise that didn't involve candy at all. The important thing was that, by making that compromise, I had begun to teach my child that there were ways of finding satisfaction other than whining and begging, and I had begun to teach myself that there were ways to deal with whining and begging other than seething inside and eventually blowing up.

A power struggle is usually evident too in an argument between a husband and wife. The process of bargaining for mutual profit which I mentioned in chapter 5 is simply a grownup version of the problem-solution method I have described. By now you may have tried mutual profit bargaining and registered either some success or a discouraging failure. If you've been successful, I encourage you to keep with it. Dealing with others in a mature and effective way isn't like riding a bicycle — you *can* forget how, and quickly. Keep practicing, evaluating, and improving your communication skills.

If you've tried and met with some discouragement, re-evaluate. Remember the steps? Express your feelings (un-embellished with judgments or decrees); avoid being defensive (when you feel you need to defend yourself you can be sure you are on the short end of a power struggle); listen to your husband with sensitivity and real concern; then begin the problem-solving process. Identify the problem, brainstorm for possible solutions, and arrive at one which will be mutually profitable.

If your husband has appeared defensive as you've made your attempt at problem solving it may be that he feels that he should be the one to introduce the new approaches, or that he doesn't like to play follow-the-leader unless he's the leader. This is a classic example of the husband-wife power contest. Many parent education groups refuse to admit a wife without a husband, or a husband without a wife, because they are concerned that one will try to change the communication pattern and the other will resist. This can be a problem, especially when one insists on change in behavior from the other. Insisting, as you will recall, was on the list of parent power-struggle behaviors.

As you attempt to change your behavior toward your husband, remember this: You have the authority to change your own behavior, but you do not have the right to control his. If he resists, cool it for a while. Avoid even the appearance of a power struggle! But you can still work on making yourself less defensive and less insisting. Integrate these ground rules into your own defense or offense the next time you have a confrontation:

1. *Don't hit below the belt.* If you have been married for very long, you have undoubtedly discovered your husband's Achilles heel, his areas of vulnerability. If you've developed your fighting powers, you may have formed the habit of going for the weak spots. It may take months, even years, to break this habit, but do it. Only then will there be hope of elevating your "fights" to the level of problem-solving sessions.

2. *Never drive your opponent against the wall or get him in a corner.* You may feel that you've won when you've so overpowered your opponent that he has no comeback, no defense. But what have you won? Nothing worth having; but you do have a very frustrated opponent who is desperate enough to forget all the rules of fair fighting and come out swinging frantically. You may get hurt in that way!

3. *Be sure you understand your opponent's goal*, or the purse he's competing for, by giving feedback frequently. To be sure you are interpreting him correctly, practice the re-

flective listening we talked about in chapter 8. Instead of that snappy comeback to an accusation, try to determine exactly what the problem is, and test your interpretation. "What I think you are saying is...." You may find that you are both striving for the same goal but that your communication is garbled. Or you may find that both of you are more able to discuss the problem rationally when the element of communication is introduced.

The first time you turn a power struggle into a problem-solving session you'll feel like celebrating. Step by step you'll become more skillful in recognizing and avoiding power struggles, and your family will thrive on the newly created atmosphere of "Every Member a Winner."

Chapter 10
The Magic Potatoes

◇○◁──────────────────────────

My children love chocolate cake. They like rich, dark brown, almost black chocolate cake with rich, thick, gooey brown frosting. They like the kind of chocolate cake that I can't eat without at least two scoops of vanilla ice cream and a quart of milk to help it go down.

My husband and I have more delicate tastes; a light Swiss chocolate with coconut pecan frosting, or a rhubarb pie, are more to our liking. But the kids hate coconut and rhubarb, so to satisfy us all I usually bake chocolate chip cookies.

This week we got the flu. Not the swine flu or Victoria flu, type A or B, which might have qualified us for complete bed rest or even hospitalization; just the plain old mid-winter virus that we have labeled "The Seven-day Blahs." First my son, then my daughter started out with the headache and fever, the chills and the cough, and the ill temper which can be bad news when a brother and sister two years apart are sentenced to stay in the same house and share the same TV set for a week of school days. In proper motherly fashion, I couldn't decide whether I had the flu or not. You know how it is: you never get sick enough to get out of any work, but you never feel well enough to really keep up. So what does all this have to do with chocolate cake?

I had been asked to bake a cake for the Cub Scout banquet and to provide dessert for a family in the ward. I searched through the few commodities left in my "year's supply" after a busy Christmas season and a few confining snowstorms, and found a couple of chocolate cake mixes. I mixed them together and divided them into a sheet cake pan and two layer pans. Not wishing to crowd the oven, I baked the sheet cake first.

Soon the house was filled with the rich, thick aroma of dark brown chocolate. My daughter, looking positively pitiful in her pink pajamas and red and blue print bathrobe, appeared in the kitchen doorway. As she spied the two chocolate layers sitting on the kitchen table the dark hollows in her face began to resume the gleam they'd had before the advent of the virus, and her face broke into her irresistible smile. "Oh, Mom!" she beamed. "My favorite!"

I explained to her that one was for the Cub Scouts and the other was for the Johnsons. She shuffled back into her room, her eyes again dark hollows, her cheeks sunken. By this time the fumes had reached the second bedroom. My son came bounding into the kitchen with his bedspread wrapped around him like an Indian blanket. He hugged me hard, oblivious of our mutual shooting pains.

"It's for the blue and gold banquet," I said apologetically. He looked hopefully at the two uncooked layers on the table. "They're for the Johnsons." He coughed dramatically and trudged back to bed.

I could have delivered a sermon about the blessings of sacrifice, but somehow I don't think that would have been right. In the past I'd always doubled the recipe when I'd baked something for a Church function or for a friend; in the future I'll continue to do so. The joy of giving has to come before a healthy sense of sacrifice can be developed.

Years ago I read a magazine article written by a young woman, the daughter of a minister. The article was all about how resentful she had been when, as a child, she had been deprived of all treats, toys, and gifts because her father had needed all the money he could get to help the poor. I am sure this father had thought he was setting an example of un-selfishness and giving, but something went wrong. Because his giving was always directed toward the outside world and never toward his own family, his daughter had grown into a selfish, unhappy, resentful woman.

I have often thought how uncomplicated, albeit austere, life in a convent would be. In a sense, the two-year period our young men are asked to devote to missionary service shares the aspect of simplicity. The work is hard, even gruelling at times, but the decisions have something of a black-and-white quality: If you do the Lord's work you are doing right; if not, you are wrong.

In a family, decisions have less of a black-and-white quality. Often instead of asking, "Which is right and which is wrong?" we find ourselves asking, "Which is most im-portant?" There are times when giving our all to a Church auxiliary organization may conflict with giving our best to our families. As mothers, we are constantly faced with fine lines and varying shades of right.

One of the stories in my second-grade reader (yes, chil-dren, they *did* have real books when Mother went to school!) was about some magic potatoes. You've heard the theme — a family shared the last food they had with a poor hungry traveler, and as a gift of appreciation the traveler left with them a bag of potatoes. Not just any old bag of potatoes, mind you — these were magic potatoes! I can remember how excited I was when I read that each time a potato was taken from the bag, another even bigger potato would come to take its place! To a second-grader, this was a thrilling idea.

I sort of grew up with the understanding that this was the way it was with love: the more you gave, the more you had. This idea became less of a beautiful abstraction and more of a mathematical problem when the parallel was again brought to my attention.

When my son was three years old it became undeniably evident that we had built our dream home in a neighborhood of teenagers and adults. Except for some six- and eight-year-old boys who came over occasionally when they had nothing better to do, there were no children at all on our street. I spent a lot of time with my son, but I knew he needed the kind of association that he could get only with other three-year-olds. I looked at a couple of nursery schools in the area but kept coming back to the same idea. A friend and I started a play group in my home.

The group grew in numbers, and we located a room in a nearby church. When my friend moved I found a new person to help me, and we grew into our own independent nursery school. I enjoyed the opportunity to do some teaching, and my children liked the abundance of playmates and play equipment. But as the size of the school grew, my responsibilities increased, and I began to wonder whether I had done the right thing.

One day I mentioned to one of the mothers that I felt I might be neglecting my own children while helping everyone else's. She answered sweetly, "Oh, you *never* run out of love."

That should be true, I thought. Love should be like the magic potatoes — the more you use, the more you have. Then didn't I love all the children? Why was I feeling pressured and put-upon?

I determined that if you think of love in terms of a feeling, or even a sense of commitment, it is true that you never run out of love. But if you think of love in terms of showing love by the things you do, your love can only last as long as the time you have to give to it. I might love my children, but if I didn't have time to play with them, or listen to them, or rock them, how would they profit from my love? So to all those pretty, ethereal ideas of love (love is blind, love is not having to say you're sorry, love is eternal . . .) I had to be practical and add the one I had found to be most dependable: "Love is something that demands a whole lot of time."

I was disappointed when the good and wise man in white, addressing bride and groom friends of mine in the Salt Lake Temple, included "my socks and underwear folded neatly in my drawer" as proof that his wife loved him. I was young and newly married then, and of all the ways to prove love and devotion I thought socks and underwear had to be one of the least worthy of note. Now, looking back on sixteen years of marriage, I see that clean socks and underwear are a terrific way to show someone you care. And if time spent on caring is important to a husband who could, if he had to, wash his own socks and underwear, how important it is to those who depend on us for all their physical needs at first, and for their first experiences of belonging, of feeling cared about, and for their early experiences with human relationships! It takes time to change diapers and prepare formula; it takes time to apply a Bandaid and sing a lullaby. It takes time to teach responsibility and self-respect. A lot of time.

Many Latter-day Saints believe that if they put their Church responsibilities first and fulfill their Church callings the Lord will take care of their families. I have heard that philosophy so often, and from such respected sources, that I almost feel heretical in suggesting otherwise. I know there are times when the concept has to be true, as in the case of the early apostles. But as my understanding of the gospel increases, and as my judgment matures, it seems to me that for most of us that philosophy is a backward approach to right living. The Church auxiliaries were created to aid the home; there are no organizations which precede the family in eternal importance.

It is possible to live a magic potato kind of existence. There are people who live on such a high plane that they seem to have time to do more than one Church job beautifully, be a helpful counselor to anyone in need of a listening ear, provide unlimited goodies for ward functions and families with sick or just tired mothers, and provide ample love and clean laundry for their own families. These people know the meaning of never running out of love; they know the secret of the full to overflowing larder. They even find time to take piano lessons or paint paintings and occasionally to do good deeds for themselves too. To be a magic-potato type is a goal worth striving for.

The mistake many of us make, though, is in assuming that simply by spreading ourselves too thin we will attain that quality of abundance and endless ability. We don't stop to realize that we might be just plain potatoes, the kind that come in bags marked "10 pounds" and mean just that. A regular potato is limited in the amount of nourishment it can provide.

I've had brief glimpses of how it would be to be a magic-potato type. You probably have, too. It's these brief glimpses, and the memory of the warm, glowing feeling that accompanies them, that reminds us that keeping a reservoir full of love and energy is a worthwhile goal. With me, anyway, these experiences all begin in the same way: I find myself in a situation where I have to fulfill a lot of responsibilities in a limited amount of time and I realize that there is no way for me to keep all my commitments without some help. With this recognition, I inform my Heavenly Father of my predicament and ask — plead, beg — for any help he can give. Then I carry out my responsibilities in a way that outshines my usual level of performance. The responsibilities can be small or great, but the euphoria that accompanies the preparations and the carrying out of the responsibilities is always the same.

Due to my lack of skill in maintaining heights, however, eventually I sink back into the struggle to keep my head above water. I find that if I spend too much time on the phone discussing the ward's problems my laundry piles up or my kitchen cabinet becomes hidden beneath the flour and sugar and bowls and pans. I begin to feel hypocritical when my daughter remarks that she will surely be glad when I'm through giving the mother education lesson so that I will be able to help her with her CTR project. When someone breaks my strain of concentration with "Do I have any clean shirts?" I know that, no matter how much visiting teaching I may do, in no scripture does the Lord promise to provide me with household help over and above the health and strength I need to load my automatic washer.

So I have come to grips with reality. It is necessary for me to understand my limitations and consider them in my planning as I continue to try to increase my physical stamina and spiritual strength. I won't assume that I will always have as much time as I have things to do; but I will have faith that, as my desire to serve increases, so will my ability to work.

Our families shouldn't have to resent the time we spend carrying out Church responsibilities or helping others. If they do, it could mean either that (1) we need to reorder our priorities and place the needs of the family higher on the list or (2) we need to examine our own attitudes toward Church service.

Some women enjoy the social aspect of Church work and use it as a means to escape from the humdrum existence of home. They wouldn't think of working outside the home or of joining a social club, but they feel good about neglecting their home duties for the sake of the Primary, the Relief Society, or some other Church organization.

I don't mean to imply that if your house looks like a disaster area the day you give your Relief Society lesson, or if you consistently have stew or hot dogs on Primary day, you are suffering from a distorted sense of perspective. Except for those blessed few who seem to have it all under control, for most of us there are the occasional times when we have to postpone home duties in order to fulfill Church assignments. The time to start worrying is when your home begins to *constantly* look like a disaster area, or when your children resign themselves to the fact that the cookie jar and the fruit bowl are always empty, or when your husband stops being shocked when he comes home and finds the ten-year-old in charge of heating up the TV dinner while you attend another meeting. And you can suspect that your time is being mis-spent if you are missing out on the mother-child or husband-wife relationships that evolve from a family's being together with time to share.

More common than the compulsive auxiliary worker are those of us who accept a reasonable number of re-sponsibilities and fulfill our assignments admirably but not totally willingly. We would never speak disrespectfully of "the authorities" in the presence of our children, but we can't resist complaining about all our Church jobs when we talk to our best friends, or pulling a face when we tell our husbands about our latest assignment. We may even betray ourselves whenever the telephone rings, responding like a conditioned animal just as the rats in the maze respond to the flashing lights. The ringing of the phone is followed by an immediate vocal response — a tired groan. The younger children probably don't know that the ring of a telephone and a human groan are two separate sounds!

Actually, to a mother, Church work has two functions in addition to assisting her personal growth. First, of course, the job has to be done and someone has to do it. Second, although it may not be second in importance, carrying out her Church responsibilities provides a terrific vehicle for teach-ing her children right attitudes toward service. In thinking "I'll get this task out of the way so that I can do something with or for my children," we make the Church responsibility become an obstacle to family togetherness. In asking "How can this Church responsibility provide a learning activity for my family?" we begin to integrate Church service with family living. In approaching Church service in this way, we lessen the likelihood of resentment and that torn feeling that comes from trying to please too many masters.

For starters, compassionate service is an obvious area in which we can involve our children. I once read a suggestion from one of the General Authorities that we should always let our children know when we are doing something for others. It can mean so much to a child to become involved in a compassionate service project and to talk about the happiness that comes with sharing. It takes just a little more time to make a family project out of taking in a meal or making a basket for someone who is sick, and these experiences will say to your child: "It's a lot of fun helping other people; it means doing things together as a family, trying to decide what will make a certain person happy, and seeing the grateful look on his face when he sees what you have done for him. It means doing something extra that only you can do. Helping is like art and music — it is another way that we can be creative."

A pleasant experience with compassionate service is worth all the lesson objectives that "Jesus wants us to help others" that our children will come across in all their years of Sunday School and Primary, and it will provide a background for them to know what the Church youth service projects are really for. Yet it is so easy to miss these opportunities by saying: "Keep out of the kitchen, will you? I've got an extra dinner to prepare tonight, and I'm in a hurry!"

By seeing us carry out our Church responsibilities, our children are forming their own attitudes. It's hard to put on an act; as my children grow more perceptive I am finding that it's imperative that I come to grips with my Church calling and learn to carry it out in an attitude of joy and giving. We are very careful to teach our children to love their Father in heaven, to help them gain a testimony of the gospel, to teach them correct principles. Then, when we are hit with an unexpected assignment or pressured under an uncomfortable deadline, we often let our discouragement show in a way that says: "Church work is a real drag. You do it because you are afraid of punishment or feeling guilty if you don't, and you do a good job because you have some pride in yourself. You have to *do* it, but you don't have to *enjoy* it!''

Church work (and the problems and blessings which accompany it) means different things to different people. For most of our married life my husband and I have lived in small wards, where to be in a presidency meant to fill, at least on a temporary basis, many of the positions in the organization, and where to have only one calling meant that you weren't doing your fair share. We have lived in a situation where the extended family meant parents in one state and brothers and sisters in still another, and where the opportunity for compassionate service was limitless. On the other hand, I listen to my cousin in Utah tell about her ward, where visiting teachers are excited when someone has a baby because at last they will get a chance to take in the proverbial two meals; and I remember my Brigham Young University wards where they created positions like "Sacrament Bread Coordinator" and "Hymn Book Distributor" to make sure that everyone had an opportunity to serve. Some of us tend to feel bogged down and defensive when the load becomes greater than we think it should be; others feel insulted because they are not given enough to do. Some seek after "high" positions; others seek not to be noticed.

Our Church leaders give us direction and instructions; and I do not presume to add to or detract from these. In addition, just as each ward, each individual, each family is unique, each set of circumstances must be viewed in its own light.

One fact stands out clearly: *No one else can fill your position as wife and mother*. This has to be a guide as we make decisions regarding priorities. But in addition to the responsibilities of wifehood and motherhood, each of us must carry some responsibility for the functioning of our ward and/or stake. For years I have struggled with the questions: "How much Church activity is enough?" "How can I lose myself in the service of others without losing all sense of the private inner-self I value?" For years I found myself torn and dissatisfied. I finally concluded that I would never find the answers because I was asking the wrong questions.

In something close to desperation I finally turned to my Father in heaven. I'll admit that subconsciously I might have harbored the ridiculous hope that he would answer by handing down a written excuse from all auxiliary positions for a given period of time so that I might put my house in order and do some of the things I had always wanted to do for myself. But guess what! Instead of such a cop-out, I found that the only solution to my problem lay in the surrender of my "limited nourishment" lifestyle to an all-out attempt to become a "magic potato" type. Tired, run-down me, who goes to sleep at 10:00 P.M. no matter where I am or what I am doing!

With this answer I was given a little encouragement and insight, perhaps to help ease the burden. A little stride-lengthening, mixed with increased dependence on my Father in heaven and a concentrated effort toward peace with myself (my real self, not the follow-the-pattern-in-ten-easy-steps type of woman I used to think I had to be), is bringing the picture of myself as an abundant fountain of energy into some semblance of focus. I'll probably use every minute of the eternity I've been promised before I actually find the winning combination that leads to never running out of love, or time, or energy; but if from time to time I can just catch a glimpse of myself as happy, un-uptight, giving, and loving, there is hope.

Until I am transformed into that munificent woman, I'm trying hard to develop those not-so-poetic but oh, so necessary traits of character, common sense and the ability to work. With or without magic, you can't go wrong with these.

Chapter 11
We're All in
This Thing Together

◇◦◁————————————————————

As I write, it's the winter of 1976-77, and all of us in the eastern United States, having previously grown used to whatever degree of comfort we can afford, are suddenly trying to train our bodies to feel comfortable in a 65-degree house and two or three layers of clothing. It has been a colder winter than usual and the rumors of natural gas shortages have suddenly turned into cold, frightening, realities. The Florida fruit has frozen. On the other side of the continent the western states are unable to enjoy their clear blue skies and mild weather because of the scarcity of water. People in New York and Ohio have been deluged with snow and some literally frozen to death, while California cities have become parched in the sun.

The strange behavior of the winter weather is a reminder that none of us are exempt from the possibility of disaster. While it would be destructive to dwell on the various accidents or illnesses that are within the realm of possibility, it might be wise for each of us to take an inventory of her emotional first-aid kit to be sure we are as prepared as possible to handle any catastrophes, large or small, which might occur.

Death, illness, and accident can provide a real challenge to the inner workings of a family. I read of a research team which had studied the families of children who suffered from leukemia. They found an extremely high incidence of alcoholism, divorce, and emotional breakdowns among parents of children with this fatal disease. The inference was that families couldn't cope with the intense emotional demands that facing such a situation involved.

Just as overwhelming are the emotional traumas that more and more families are having to face: a divorce; an excommunication; a daughter's announcement that she is pregnant, though she is so very young and so very single; a child's rejection of his parents' teachings and his alignment with friends and habits which the parents cannot accept. These situations often awaken the same feelings of grief in families as do purely physical ailments, although added feelings of guilt or blame can add intensity to the emotional pain.

Loss of employment, moving, children's school problems, and parents' adjustment problems also can cause a sense of shock and insecurity within a family. Any drastic change in lifestyle, such as a promotion which suddenly changes the home-by-the-fire-at-six father into a leave-on-Monday, home-on-Friday traveler, can throw a family into a spin.

Recently medical doctors, psychologists, and ministers have given much attention to the need for helping patients and their families to deal with problems accompanying the imminent death of the patient. They have identified the stages one goes through when he finds he has a fatal disease.

In every sudden trauma there is a period of adjustment. We don't suddenly accept the loss of a loved one, or an illness, or a handicap as part of our lives without a rearrangement of our thoughts and feelings. In this chapter I have borrowed from the stages which have been identified as parts of the process of accepting a fatal illness and have adapted them to show the stages we go through when faced with any major misfortune.

The first reaction to the onset of any problem which is difficult to face is denial. "There must be some mistake!" "The Lord wouldn't let this happen to me!" At this stage our minds refuse to accept the impact of what has happened or what inevitably has to happen. This is a very human, very normal reaction. But it is normal only to the extent that it is a transitory stage.

There are some facts which obviously cannot be denied. While a patient can choose not to believe a medical diagnosis or a mother can deny that her child is taking drugs, a rational person who has evidence of the fact that a family member has died or met with an accident cannot deny that fact. But a numbness, an inability to feel the impact of a death or disaster, seems to accompany traumas of this nature. It is as if our bodies and emotional systems were spontaneously given a shot of Novocain to numb us until we become prepared to deal with the reality of the loss.

At some point in the process of acceptance it is a common experience to feel anger. This is the stage at which so many people ask, "Why me, Lord?" or "What did I do to deserve this?" Anger can be directed toward the Lord, for letting it happen, or toward the person who caused the grief. Sometimes anger is felt even toward a loved one who has died, or in other words has gone on without you. But anger, too, should subside in time. We must also allow time for a period of mourning or grief.

The stages of denial, then anger, are especially obvious in a divorce. A woman I know was convinced for weeks that her husband had asked for a divorce impulsively, that he would soon come to his senses and reconsider. When she finally came to the conclusion that it was "for real," she experienced an overwhelming feeling of anger, recognizing feelings of hostility she never could have imagined she could feel. Eventually the anger subsided as she moved on to the next stage of acceptance.

Some people try to deny the stage of anger, rationalizing that it is not good to feel angry. People may also try to escape the stage of grief, arguing that it is weak to cry or it is self-indulgent to grieve. While it is true that any of these stages, if carried out for a long period or totally surrendered to, can prove destructive, it is also true that to refuse to acknowledge the feelings in any of the stages can cause harm. When I do my laundry, if I set the dial at the beginning of the cycle and let it run its course the clothes will be clean and free from detergent at the end of the cycle. If, however, I move the dial and skip one of the steps, I can't blame my washer if the clothes are still dirty, or are stiff from inadequate rinsing. By accepting each stage as it comes, by understanding that our feelings are not abnormal and by knowing that they will pass, we are allowing ourselves to participate in a cleansing process that can roughly be compared with the process we put our clothes through when we wash them. By refusing to accept one of the steps, we refuse to let the cleansing take place, and we make it difficult for ourselves ever to come to the point of acceptance of the loss or resolution of the problem.

Strength and bravery are great qualities, but true strength is developed through an acceptance of natural laws and the fortification of spirit that comes from living in accordance with those laws. It is not weak to allow yourself to grieve at the loss of someone you love, but it is weak to be so engulfed in grief that you refuse eventually to look forward to the time when the grief will have passed. Children must be taught that a period of mourning is acceptable. Don't encourage your child to "be brave, now, don't cry . . ." when his puppy is run over or when his friend moves to another city. We accept an increase in body temperature when we are ill; we should as readily accept the methods our body provides for us to adjust to traumatic events.

It is true that, because of our religious beliefs as Latter-day Saints, death does not have the aspect of hopelessness and finality that can be overwhelming. It is comforting to know that death is simply the passing of a spirit from one realm to another. The comforting powers of the Holy Ghost, too, can be of tremendous help in times of bereavement. Nevertheless, regardless of one's beliefs about life after death, death of a loved one is a loss; and at such times a certain amount of shock and grief is natural and appropriate.

It is important that we allow our children to understand the finality of death. Sometimes children get confused with all the talk about resurrection and wonder why, if Grandpa's spirit is still alive, he doesn't come back and visit. When I did my student teaching in a special class at the University of Utah the supervising teacher asked me to plan a special unit of study about death, because the child for whom the unit was to be planned had lost an aunt and he was obsessed with the idea that she would come out of the grave and return to them. His family had put so much emphasis on the fact that she would live again that they had failed to help him understand physical death.

A friend related a story which shows the ease with which a child who doesn't understand death can misinterpret our attempts to make the death of a loved one easier by focusing on the resurrection. Teresa was nearly three when her father was killed in a traffic accident. Her mother, through her own strength of character and the strength she had gained from her Father in heaven, had been able to sit down with Teresa and her brother and explain to them that their father would no longer be able to live on earth with them, but that he had gone to live with Heavenly Father, in His house. Teresa's brother understood, and he mourned the death of his father, but Teresa seemed to accept her father's absence without a second thought.

Later, Teresa's grandmother, noticing the child's apparent obliviousness to the sense of loss, asked Teresa if she knew why her daddy wasn't with them. "Oh, yes," she answered cheerfully. "He's gone to Primary!" To her, the words "Heavenly Father's house" elicited only one image — the brick edifice in which they had so often attended meetings together.

After we have experienced the periods of denial or numbness, anger, and grief, and allowed ourselves to recognize and accept these feelings, normally there will come a time when we are ready, even anxious, to go on with the business of living. Eventually, if we have admitted our feelings and been honest with ourselves, we will find the peace of mind we need to accept the inevitable (as in the case of a death or a problem over which we have no control), to work toward a solution to a problem, or to develop an alternate plan.

When a trauma is more acute for one member of the family than another, husbands and wives can have a tremendous strengthening influence on one another, and even children can provide a source of inspiration and encouragement. The most difficult situations arise when a death, serious illness, injury, or emotional upheaval occurs within the immediate family. Then Father, Mother, and children are all affected personally, and often one member of the family will look to another for support, only to find that that person too is in need of emotional first aid.

They used to tell us, at those programs they put on to help girls prepare to be good wives and mothers, that it was the woman who set the emotional atmosphere of the home. I had thought that was another one of the things they said to flatter us into living exemplary lives. What I then thought was a pretty compliment I find now to be a frightening responsibility. In my own home, at least, I have found it to be undeniably true that when I am optimistic, level-headed, and in control of my emotions my family is happy and able to cope with whatever problems come up. On the other hand, when I am "down" the family follows the example and allows everyday problems to become catastrophes. Does this mean, then, that in a family trauma Mother must ignore her feelings of grief and anger and simply try to administer to the needs of the other family members?

Because she is responsible for the emotional climate of the home it is even more important that Mother accept, rather than ignore, the normal period of mourning.[1] The natural tendency for a mother is to protect her offspring, to shield her children from painful realities. Sometimes, though, children need to be educated to deal with reality rather than protected from it. Have you ever had the feeling that something is going on, but you can't figure out what it is? I get almost a paranoiac feeling even in those party games where I am sent out of the room and everyone knows the secret but me, and I am supposed to figure out what the secret is. I am sure this is how a child must feel when he is being shielded from the truth of a family crisis. He knows there is a problem; he is suffering the tension and the fear without the benefit of knowing what the problem is.

Some mothers, when faced with a tragedy such as the death of a loved one, a divorce, or the serious illness or adjustment problem of another child, will send a child away to stay with a friend or relative to shield him from the impact of the problem. If the mother is totally unable to deal with the situation herself this may, of course, be the only solution. But being sent away from home can add a feeling of rejection to the fear and confusion already worrying the child who sees the results of a problem but not the problem itself.

The most compassionate thing we can do when there is a problem within the immediate family is to make sure that each child understands as well as he can, depending upon his own degree of maturity, the problem and its implications. A

---

[1]The word *mourning* here is used to describe the reaction to any traumatic occurrence, not only death.

mother need not be ashamed of having her children see her going through any of the normal stages of acceptance, for that is the way children learn that it is all right for *them* to go through these stages. Of course children should be shielded from any irrational reactions to tragedy, or from extreme emotional outbreaks. But having a good cry together, talking about feelings of denial, anger, and grief, are ways of saying: "We are sharing hard times as we share good times. The hurt is real, but it will go away."

It may be even more difficult to share family crises with a husband than with a child. We have been conditioned to expect certain behaviors from men and certain other behaviors from women. A husband is always supposed to provide a strong shoulder to cry on; a wife is always supposed to provide warmth and tenderness. When the husband is crushed by a sudden loss and cannot provide the strength that is expected of him, or when he is so determined to prove his own strength that he becomes cold and brittle, the wife may find her grief multiplied because her primary source of comfort has let her down. When a wife is so stricken with her own grief that she is unable to provide warmth and tenderness to a hurting husband, the husband may find his burden too great to bear. And when the problem in question is one of a rebellious child, the ability to offer comfort to one another may be hampered to an even greater degree by blaming the other ("If you had been there when she needed you, this wouldn't have happened!") or by blaming oneself ("If I had spent more time with him, he wouldn't have had to go to such lengths to get attention!"). At such times we need the help of the Lord, and perhaps an objective outsider, to help us not to make matters worse by allowing the problem to produce a marital chasm which may remain even after the pain of the existent problem has subsided.

Families can provide a source of comfort or a source of frustration as they face crises together. No member of the family can remain unaffected by such crises; each member can be strengthened if, through a determined effort to sustain an atmosphere of love and support, parents and children accept their own feelings and show concern for the feelings of others. In this sense, "We're All in This Thing Together."

In a broader sense, all of us can lend support to members of our extended families, our ward families, and fellow members of the universal fraternity we call "the brotherhood of man," when such support is needed. You might be the one who can communicate with a young girl who feels that the lines of communication are permanently closed between herself and her parents. You might be able to help a friend through a crisis simply by providing an understanding soundingboard for her thoughts. By recognizing the woman who comes to church in a wheelchair as "the woman with the quick sense of humor" instead of as "the handicapped sister," you might begin to free her from the prison that others have created.

You can help, too, by withholding judgment on those who are experiencing periods of family instability, Church inactivity, or parent-child conflict. This business of educating the eternal family was never supposed to be easy, or painless, or free from opposition. Most growing pains do not occur in the bones or muscles, but rather in the heart.

Chapter 12
Hold Tight and Hang Loose

"They are the loosest yet the straightest kids I know!" My sister threw me a curve by her description of my nephew and his wife. I couldn't see how "straightness" and "looseness" could be compatible.

I was similarly puzzled many years ago when my bishop suggested: "You can't take your Church job too seriously. You can take *yourself* too seriously, though."

Straight, uncompromising, singleminded. These are the qualities I had always associated with goodness. And what was wrong with taking myself too seriously? Being a self is serious business!

Perhaps one of the reasons why we are commanded to be parents and are given children is that in parenting we are put in a position where we must learn that flexibility, acceptance, and the ability to compromise (in the best sense of that term) are facets of the celestial personality along with the more obvious ones. In parenting, we *may* learn these principles only after all else has failed. We may be like the teenager in Oregon who stood up in testimony meeting and said, in all sincerity, "I know that the only way to gain a testimony of the gospel is through study and prayer, because I've tried every other way and it *doesn't work!*''

We see vividly the need for both "straightness" and "looseness" in cases where a child has rebelled against the teachings of his parents. The parents sense that they have lost control of the child, but they are not willing to give up. They go to the bishop, and perhaps they are told to "straighten up"; to put their lives in order, to be more faithful and prayerful. Or they go to the family counselor and are told to "loosen up"; to try to relax and improve the climate at home; to be willing to compromise in an attempt to improve communication.

We see the principles of "straightness" and "looseness" juxtaposed in marriage, too. Until the right balance has been established, marriage can be, as I once heard it described, "an insane institution."

One of my husband's friends came out of a priesthood meeting discouraged and frustrated. The lesson had been about presiding over a righteous home; and, as our friend's wife was a nonmember and was quite resentful of his Church activity, our friend asked his priesthood leader for some specific advice to apply to his situation. "Live the gospel," the leader suggested. "If you do that, everything will eventually turn out all right." Unsatisfied, our friend insisted that he had been living the gospel all his life and that it seemed that the more active in the Church he became, the more the situation at home worsened. To him, living the gospel meant the straight and narrow — Church activity, living the Word of Wisdom, honoring the Sabbath, and so on.

What he had needed was not a general, all-inclusive answer to his question but an understanding audience and some guidance toward the more benevolent aspects of the gospel — the Christ-like attributes of forgiveness, acceptance, and unconditional love. He had developed his "straightness," and that would continue to work to his eternal advantage. When he reached the point at which he could cherish "straightness" as concerning his own expectations of himself but practice "looseness" to the extent that he could become non-judgmental and facilitating toward his family, he would probably begin to see some of the rewards that were promised along with the admonition to "live the gospel."

The advice to "hold tight and hang loose" can also be tremendously helpful to the woman who is finding it difficult to fit into the niche that has been carved for her and labeled "LDS Woman." Let me mention my own experience in this respect:

In one aspect, I was a late bloomer. I grew up in the period of time they now refer to as "The Nothing Generation"; I was in high school and college in the late fifties and early sixties, when decorating for a school dance or being an officer in a social unit was more important than demonstrating for a cause. I found no reason to rebel against my parents or the Church; and, although I'm sure I caused my parents a few wrinkles and grey hairs they could have done without, I basically fitted the pattern of the conforming teenager and young adult.

Not until I was in my late twenties and early thirties did I begin to resent some of the stereotypes I had learned to accept unquestioningly. Not that I left the Church or boycotted meetings or such. I rebelled in ridiculous little ways, like refusing to bring Cheerios in Tupperware containers or quiet books to church for my children. It was the stereotype I objected to, not the eating or playing. I might bring a cookie in a Baggie, or a set of rubber toys, but *no* Tupperware or Cheerios!

The silly thing about a prejudice is that it is usually based on an inability to achieve a sense of belonging or else a need to feel superior, and its premises may be imaginary. I have heard many Mormon women say that they resented the pressure to fit into the Mormon Woman image, but probably, if I should ask them just what the Mormon Woman image was, they would all give a somewhat different answer. My Mormon Woman image was mixed up with my Suburban Woman image and included a lot of conformity (and some intolerance for nonconformists).

I heard a story once that illustrates the conformity I'm talking about.

One of the quickest hot-lines in the world is the one between Relief Society homemaking directors. Remember when everyone was making the glass grapes? They were being made in Salt Lake City, and I saw them in Champaign, Illinois, and later in Atlanta, Georgia. They were really gorgeous creations, made, I think, from melted marbles, and used to decorate homes. As for making some myself, somehow I was never in the right ward at the right time, but my friends all had them and I admired them. Then I heard the story of a woman in Salt Lake City who didn't belong to the Church. One day she asked her Mormon friend, in all seriousness and confidence: "What is the religious significance of those grapes? I have seen them in every LDS home I've been into in the Valley, so they must have something important to do with your beliefs."

Looking back I find, surprisingly, that I have been most spiritual when engaged in quite unstereotyped activities. For example, I was dismayed when I found myself married two, three, four, then five years without a baby. I needed a new challenge, so I quit teaching, obtained a research assistantship, and became a student again. I found graduate school to be the answer to my state of discontent and self-pity, although I had a hard time with the concept that I was not fitting into the picture of fruitful wife and mother that I had so carefully painted on the grey canvas of my mind. Notwithstanding, I went into the school experience with an enthusiasm and a promise to succeed that I hadn't had in high school or college. I wanted to learn everything I could — I wanted to get the best grades I could. I worked hard, and I loved it.

Our ward in Athens, Georgia, was a tiny one then. I was in the M.I.A. presidency, which meant that I also taught the Laurel class (one girl) and occupied the position of drama director. I also taught a Sunday School class. I knew I needed my Heavenly Father's help to keep me ahead of my responsibilities, and I was always asking him for favors.

I can remember clearly two instances in which my prayers were answered, I thought, miraculously. They had to do with the two hardest classes (and lowest-grading professors) in my whole course of study. In the first instance, I was taking an education course and it was the end of the fall quarter. In addition to my other tests, I had a huge report to write and a final to take on Tuesday. Being the kind of person who always finds work piled up at the last minute, I was weighted down with work by Sunday. I had strong feelings against studying on Sunday, so I decided that on Sunday I'd go to church, write my Christmas cards, offer a few *very* sincere prayers, and rest *hard* so that I could face the big week ahead. This I did.

On Monday I wrote my report as if I were writing a letter to my mother; the words came easily and freely. I made my deadline, but I had little time to study for the test. This particular professor was known for her impossible tests, so I brushed up on those things I was sure she would ask, and I asked my Father in heaven to help me to remember what I had learned during the class lectures. The test was an essay type, and again I wrote quickly and easily. The next day my instructor called me in to say that I had made the highest score in the class, by some margin. I was delighted, but not surprised.

The next time I felt that I was a recipient of a miracle, or series of miracles, was when my one Laurel and I decided we would do a roadshow. Athens had never had a roadshow before, and Sherry, my Laurel, had always wanted to participate in one. The presentation of the roadshow, I found, was inopportunely to be at the end of the quarter, when reports were due and tests had to be taken. I was taking an individual

testing course which frightened me to death, because anything that had to do with statistics and record-keeping seemed
to have a paralyzing effect on my mind. I guess the Lord was
aware that I had bitten off more than I could chew by myself,
because he was always there when I needed help.

The first crisis came when the deadline for the roadshow
script and a mammoth report for my testing class came at the
same time. I knew that I only had time to write either the
script or the report. I knew that if I messed up on the report I
would only be hurting myself, but if I messed up on the script
I would be letting down all the kids in the Athens ward. I did
the script. I won't say that I was inspired in my writing,
because it was quite a corny story about the old football
rivalry between Georgia and Georgia Tech, but the kids were
pleased with it.

I must have sacrificed a night's sleep, because somehow I
finished the report on time too. Barely. The report was due to
be in my instructor's office at noon that day. I got done at
11:45, drove to the campus, and someone considerately left a
parking space near the office building just as I arrived. I
parked and got out of the car, completely out of breath — and
realized that I didn't have any money for the parking meter!
A policeman was coming toward my meter. Without my
saying anything, he emptied the coins from the meter and
said to me, "Here, I'll give you fifteen minutes." Then he
turned the meter from the big red "Violation" sign to a
fifteen-minute reading. I laid my report on the instructor's
desk at one minute before twelve.

The entire M.I.A., as it was called then — all ten of them
— were praying for help with the roadshow. We prayed that
we would find something to use for goal posts, and on my
way home from school the next day I saw two long, narrow
bamboo poles in Sears' trash pile. We prayed that we could
find something to use for helmets, and the local war surplus
store happened to have just the right number — cheap. I

prayed that what time and effort I managed to spend on my studies would be enough, and again, for the second time in my life, I got the highest score in the class on a final exam. This time it was in my individual testing class, and I was stunned! It is my belief that that "highest in the class" was thrown in just in case I had any doubts about the heavenly assistance, because even in subjects that I found easy I had never before, and have never since, received the highest score on any test.

So much for the spiritual effect of my unstereotyped activities, which I have deliberately described in some detail. On the other hand, I hit my spiritual low at the time when I was trying very hard to remake myself into my image of the Ideal Mormon Woman. Only after realizing that there was no mold for the ideal Mormon woman, that living the gospel didn't have anything to do with quiet books or Tupperware or glass grapes or all thinking the same thoughts — only then was I able again to see my LDS sisters as the individual, fascinating, unique creations they are.

I have found that the same hold-tight, hang-loose principles hold true whether I am dealing with my husband, my children, or my sisters, in or out of the Church. On the assumption that those principles have merit for the lives of other people too, let me crystallize them like this:

Hold fast to your own spirituality — daily prayer (the real, nitty gritty, bare-your-soul kind of prayer, not the bless-the-poor-sick-needy-and-afflicted type); scripture reading; meditation; and physical fitness (yes, physical fitness is an important facet of spirituality too, for me anyway). These all help.

Hold fast to those special gifts and personality traits which set you apart from everyone else, for these are the things that make you You. Be proud of them. Cherish them. But never use them as exemptions from the need to obey the commandments of God.

Hold fast to those you love; not through control, but through warmth, acceptance, and understanding. And hold fast to a sense of perspective and a sense of humor, which will allow you to hang loose on those paralyzing prejudices, judgments, and trivialities.

Because that's what love is all about.